Contents

Foreword   *by Alex Rodriguez*   vii

Praise for *Real Estate Riches*   ix

Acknowledgments   xiii

Preface: I Don't Have a Job. Shame!   xv

PART ONE   **Why Is Property So Good?**   **1**

CHAPTER 1   Four Magic Questions   3

CHAPTER 2   Conspiracy Theory   19

CHAPTER 3   A Taxing Issue   27

CHAPTER 4   Beating the Averages Easily   33

CHAPTER 5   Yes, But . . .   63

CHAPTER 6   Summary: Why Invest in Real Estate?   69

PART TWO   **Okay! Show Me How to Do It!**   **71**

CHAPTER 7   The 100:10:3:1 Rule   73

CHAPTER 8   Finding Properties   81

CHAPTER 9   Analyzing Deals   101

CHAPTER 10   Negotiations and Submitting Offers   109

CHAPTER 11   Getting High on Opium (aka OPM)   119

CHAPTER 12   Massively Increase the Value of Your
                        Properties (Without Spending
                        Much Money)   129

CHAPTER 13   Managing Your Properties   137

PART THREE   **Liftoff!**   **149**

CHAPTER 14   Residential versus
                        Commercial Property   151

CHAPTER 15   Government Interference   169

CHAPTER 16   The Eight Golden Rules of Property   173
CHAPTER 17   The World Is Your Oyster   181

Appendix: Other Books by Dolf de Roos   187
About the Author   189
Index   191

REAL ESTATE
RICHES

REAL ESTATE
RICHES

How to Become Rich
Using Your
Banker's Money

Dolf de Roos, Ph.D.

WILEY

John Wiley & Sons, Inc.

Published by John Wiley & Sons, Inc., Hoboken, New Jersey.
Published simultaneously in Canada.

For general information on our other products and services please contact our
Customer Care Department within the United States at (800) 762-2974, outside the
United States at (317) 572-3993 or fax (317) 572-4002.

Wiley also publishes its books in a variety of electronic formats. Some content that
appears in print may not be available in electronic books. For more information about
Wiley products, visit our web site at www.wiley.com.

Library of Congress Cataloging-in-Publication Data:
De Roos, Dolf.
   Real estate riches : how to become rich using your banker's money /
Dolf de Roos.—[New ed.]
     p. cm.
   Originally published: New York : Warner Books, 2001.
   Includes index.
   ISBN 0-471-71180-2 (pbk. : alk. paper)
   1. Real estate investment. 2. Real estate investment—Finance. 3. Mortgage
loans. I. Title.
HD1382.5.D47 2004
332.63'24—dc22   2004058398

Printed in the United States of America.

10   9   8   7   6   5   4   3   2   1

Foreword

Baseball has blessed me with a sensational career and an avenue to reap rich financial rewards. However, the hard work does not stop in the baseball diamond, nor does it end with the paychecks. I am acutely aware that many professional athletes are paid well for their talents but, sadly, are victims of poor financial planning.

When I landed my well-publicized 10-year, $252 million contract, I set about finding an investment vehicle that would ensure my financial fitness long after baseball. I read many books on wealth, entrepreneurship, and investing, as well as biographies of successful individuals, but nothing inspired or captivated me as much as *Real Estate Riches* by Dolf de Roos. Dolf makes real estate investing simple and accessible to anyone who has the will to succeed. He is an All Star in his field!

On my journey to verify the opportunities available in real estate, I met with Joanne Mitchell, a good friend and local real estate advisor who owns and operates several thousand apartments in Miami. She immediately recognized the copy of *Real Estate Riches* under my arm and consequently pulled *her* copy out from her desk. Her book had been highlighted, and notes had been scribbled in the margins—it had been an inspiration to her as well. This book holds powerful recipes for prosperity.

I had to meet this wizard of real estate called Dolf de Roos. After great effort due to scheduling conflicts, we met in Dallas. To his surprise I was a baseball player and *not* a basketball player, and to my surprise he was accessible and eager to teach a newcomer his strategies. Clearly whether you are on the baseball field or a field slated for real estate investing, life is a numbers game. Some days you score big, and others, well . . .

you don't; but if you practice hard, learn from your mistakes, stay focused, and above all have passion, then the numbers start to work in your favor and your success fuels even more success.

I credit *Real Estate Riches* and Dolf de Roos as valuable guides that helped give me the confidence to form Newport Property Ventures. I began by investing in a small duplex in an emerging area of South Florida, which led to the acquisition of several other income-producing properties. With hard work and determination my projects and portfolio continue to grow with phenomenal returns. Dolf's principles are working strong!

That Dolf has passion is apparent from the first few pages of this book. This passion and enthusiasm for his game is even more apparent when you meet him in person. Recently we met in New York where we once again reviewed the principles that lead to great success in a newfound sport from which I will never have to retire!

—Alex Rodriguez, #13
M.L.B. American League MVP
Founder and CEO, Newport Property Ventures

August 2004

Praise for *Real Estate Riches*

"I have always been interested in property but have never had the courage to admit to myself that property is in fact a passion of mine and not just an interest. Your book, *Real Estate Riches*, has helped me make that final leap and as a result I have decided to pursue my passion and restructure my life to make more time for real estate investment."

—Paul Dinis, South Africa

"I read your book, *Real Estate Riches*, and I loved it. Thanks for breaking things down in such a simple fashion. I am now looking to get into real estate investing."

—Mike Desroches, New York

"I just closed my first Las Vegas property last week and want to thank you for pointing me in the right direction and giving me the tools to begin my investing. I feel like I have begun building my real estate dynasty! I am very happy; thank you so much!!!!!!!!"

—Pamela, California

"Thank you so much for the great book *Real Estate Riches*."

—Moshe Mizrachi, California

"I have read Dr. Dolf de Roos' book titled *Real Estate Riches*. Two weeks ago I bought my first rental flat, then a week later my first rental building (six flats). It's magic to create wealth out of thin air. Thank you for your inspiring books."

—L.C., France

"I bought your book *Real Estate Riches* and your course *Property Investor's School* and used the information to buy a $1.2 million commercial building. Thanks for all of the great information. I couldn't have done the deal without the information I learned from you. I used your advice to do the deal and immediately raised the building value by $160,000."

—Sam Beckford, Vancouver, Canada

"I have just finished reading your book *Real Estate Riches*. The information was helpful and encouraging. Thanks for your willingness to share your experiences.

"Along with my partner (older sister) I am a novice investor. Six months ago, we purchased our first property, a six-unit commercial building. Last week, we made an offer on a second commercial property. So far, it is exciting work. I hope that the excitement and profits continue!"

—Mike W. Sanderson, Virginia

"I have just completed your book *Real Estate Riches*. What a great book."

—Brian Hunter, Boulder, Colorado

"I am a mother of four and awaiting my turn in 'real estate riches.' (That was a great book; I'm reading it again.) Because of the book *Real Estate Riches*, my husband and I felt bold enough to take over my parents' property (they didn't want to deal with the mortgage anymore). We refinanced, took money out, and now are in negotiations to buy an investment property. Dolf de Roos helped us to think out of the box."

—Vivienne Piña, California

"I have recently joined a real estate company and have read your book *Real Estate Riches*. I am a keen businessman, and after reading your book property makes a lot of sense. Thank you for the great inspiration."

—Rudi Maritz, South Africa

"I recently purchased one of your books (I already had *Real Estate Riches*). I just wanted to say that I am really enjoying them and I can't wait to actually get out there and utilize the principles. Thank you so much!"

—Mark Smith, Kentucky

"I just wanted to pass along a thank-you for inspiring me to start my real estate investing career. I have been successful in one jointly owned short-term rental property. I am in the process of laying the basic foundation for residential rentals and hope to own my first one June 2004.

"Out of all the real estate gurus I've listened to and read, you have reached me the most. The message I received from your books is a source of constant inspiration for me whenever I need it. I love your can-do attitude and upbeat personality. I hope you will continue to write and pass on your experiences."

—Patrick Mintel, Florida

"Just finished *Real Estate Riches* and enjoyed it very much. Can't wait to continue my search for the riches."

—Becky Moran, Erie, Pennsylvania

"I read your book *Real Estate Riches*, and found it both empowering and life changing. THANKS. You added value to my life."

—Wikus Strydom, Cape Town,
South Africa

"Thank you for your assistance. I greatly appreciate your time and the valuable information that you have bestowed upon me. This new thinking has changed the direction of my life. Thank you."

—Emily F. Henderson, California

"Dear Dolf,
I bought your books
I bought your tapes
I bought your seminar
I've made millions because of you.
Thanks. I listen, I learn, I do!"

—Steve Gronlund, California

Acknowledgments

My thoughts, theories, methods, mistakes, successes, wins, and learnings in real estate have been formulated over many years. Countless people have—wittingly or unwittingly—contributed to my thinking, from real estate agents, bankers, mortgage brokers, and appraisers to tenants, members of real estate investment associations, and thousands of investors (both budding and experienced) who have honored me by attending my events and who have forced me to expand my thinking. While it is impossible to acknowledge everyone, an array of people deserve and have my deep appreciation. If I have missed you, then I apologize in advance; know that my appreciation is real nonetheless. Sincere thanks go to Trevor Quirk, David Henderson, Mike Pero, Stephen Witte, Kevin O'Gorman, David Grose, Charles Drace, Stephen Collins, Paul Wright, Ron Whiteley, David Thompson, Allen and Kenina Court, Robert Tybon, Dr. John Baen, Diane Kennedy, Tom Wheelwright, Ann Mathis, Kim Butler, Gene Burns, Andy Fuehl, Carrie Putman, Stefan Kasian, Cindy Kenney, Claudia Brelo, Ross Denny, Randy Carder, and Andy Driggs.

On the publication front, I would like to sincerely thank my agent, Larry Jellen, for his vision and confidence. Laurie Harting and Mike Hamilton at John Wiley & Sons, Inc., are a delight to work with, as are Pam Williams and Ken Burlington at the National Association of Realtors.

Finally, I would like to thank my parents for never having told me—not even once—"You can't do that!"

I DON'T HAVE A JOB.
SHAME!

To many people, my situation would be an embarrassment and an imposition. Having no job has a stigma. Take heart: For me it is not a temporary situation. I have been this way since birth. To state it more accurately:

I have <u>never</u> had a job.

Furthermore, I have never received a single cent of government money in terms of an unemployment benefit, disability payout, hardship grant, or anything of that nature. Not a single cent.

And just to clarify, I am not a trust fund baby. One of the best things my parents ever did was to leave me to my own creative devices (not that they had a choice—I am trying to state the obvious without embarrassing my parents!).

However, never having had a job does not mean that I have never worked. On the contrary, I probably work as hard as, if not harder than, most. But in terms of receiving a wage slip or a salary payment from an employer, I have no experience at that.

Sometimes people ask me what it feels like to never have had a job. I simply don't know, because I don't know what to compare it with. It's a bit like asking someone what it's like never having traveled to Pluto. But I don't mind not knowing, as I hear a lot of people complaining about their jobs.

When I was eight years old, we were living on the Gold Coast of Australia. Back then I was already trying to figure out ways of making money. In my very first venture, I set up a candy stall on the beach. I used to buy candy wholesale at 1 cent, and sell it at 2 cents. In case you are thinking that the numbers involved are small, the profit margins were huge!

On a sunny Saturday I would sell 100 pieces of candy. That meant $1 profit. It may not sound like much, but my allowance (pocket money) was 20 cents per week, so here I had figured out a way to make five times my weekly allowance *per day*. I was rich!

I was happy until some burly officials shut down my stall. No one had complained, but there were some bureaucratic regulations about selling candy in the open.

The next day I was back on the beach with a fruit stall—the regulations did not cover fruit. I was so determined to sell my self-imposed quota of fruit that I resisted calls to come home for dinner until I had completely sold out. Years later I found out that one day, in order to get me home before dark, my father gave a stranger some coins with the request to buy my entire remaining stock of fruit, so that I would finally return home. His wisdom in not forcing me home is priceless.

Business and making money are not so much about what happens to you, or the rules that are out there, but your attitude, perseverance, and desire to succeed.

My sister and I had an upbringing rich in adventure if not material luxury. Our curiosity was never dampened, but encouraged.

My parents came through the tail end of the Depression. Their reality was that to succeed in life, you had to study hard, because by studying hard you can go to college, and at college you can get a degree, and with a degree you can get a good job, and with a good job you can build a career, and with a good career, you can have all the financial security that you could ever hope for. Education was highly prized in our home.

So it was without much thinking at all that I went to college. I had a bit of trouble deciding what to do, however. Law appealed to me, but then you would be restricted to practicing in the country where you qualify, and having travel imprinted in my DNA, I didn't want to restrict myself. I couldn't stand the sight of blood, so medicine was out. The thought of looking into people's mouths all day didn't appeal at all either. In this manner I slowly eliminated all professions. Except for engineering. So off I went to engineering school.

It was during my first year studying for a bachelor's in engineering that it dawned on me that engineers were not uniformly rich. In fact, many of them seemed quite the opposite, judging by their clothes, the clunkers that they drove, and the modest houses that they occupied. So I took it upon myself to make a study of the rich, to try to figure out what it was that they had in common.

The study lasted more than seven months. I read biographies, autobiographies, the relevant parts of encyclopedias, books, and magazines about the rich, and interviewed as many wealthy people as I could. What I found astounded me.

The rich were not uniformly young or old. Nor were they always male, or female. It did not seem to matter whether they were a firstborn, lastborn, or anywhere in between. It did not matter whether they were born into a rich family, lived in a wealthy country, immigrated from a poor country, or whether they were devoutly religious, atheist, or agnostic. In fact, after more than seven months of study, I could find only two things that the rich had in common . . .

First, almost without exception, the rich had integrity.

Their word was their honor. If they said something, you could count on it. That's not to say that if you don't have integrity you cannot get rich. But I believe that if you don't have integrity and get rich, your lack of integrity will also be part of your subsequent and almost inevitable demise. And since integrity is not purely genetic, there is a lesson in this for everyone.

The second feature that the rich uniformly had in common is that almost without exception, the rich either made their wealth, or kept their wealth, in real estate.

Upon that realization, I decided to get into property.

Things were not always easy. When I was seventeen, I looked about twelve. I am sure the first bank manager I visited to seek a mortgage thought it was a prank. (Imagine what it was like for me as a seventeen-year-old kid, trying to date a seventeen-year-old girl, and she'd also think I was twelve.) But I persevered.

Meanwhile, four years later, I got my bachelor's degree with honors. And then they said to me: "Four years for a bachelor's degree, but only one more for a master's, how about it?" So I started a master's program. And halfway through, they told me that I was doing so well that I could switch my registration from a master's to a Ph.D. I wondered why not, couldn't think of an answer, and carried on. They say there are three kinds of students: part-time, full-time, and eternal. I was the eternal kind.

But one day I finally had my doctorate in hand. I was offered a job at $32,000 a year, which at the time was a handsome salary. Unfortunately for my prospective employer, the week before I had just completed a real estate deal that netted me $35,000.

I remember thinking to myself: "Why would anyone in their right mind agree to work for forty hours a week, for forty-nine weeks of the year, turning up every morning at 8:00 A.M. and saying, 'Hello boss, here I am again, what would you like me to do today?,' when in one week you can do a deal worth $35,000 and take the rest of the year off?"

My parents, no doubt proud of my academic achievements, were, I am sure, quietly waiting for me to announce my acceptance of a job offer. But the announcement never came. I got more into property. I was involved in various business ventures. Slowly I focused more and more on real estate.

When I was in my mid-thirties, I remember visiting my parents in Europe. They picked me up at the airport, and as we were driving to their house, they commented: "Maybe you did the right thing by not having a job." I know this was a big concession, not to me, but to their belief that a job was crucial to financial success. Nonetheless, I told them that I would know that they really believed it when they could drop the word *maybe* from their comments.

Over the years, as my property activities became more visible, I was asked to share what I do, and how I do it. Articles followed, then books, and a weekly two-hour radio show on property. I have lectured on real estate in over fifteen countries, have made software available to analyze and manage property, and appeared on radio and television shows discussing the merits of real estate.

Today there are many books on real estate. Almost all are correct in what they teach (as you'll learn in this book, there is no right or wrong way!). In writing this book, I do not want to present yet another version of the mechanics of property investment. Rather, I want to do two things. First, I want to share why I think property is so astoundingly simple and lucrative. I want to show property from a new perspective, so that whether you are new to the game or a seasoned investor, you will be forced to rethink how you feel about real estate. And second, I want to give you an insider's view of my approach, my attitudes, my techniques, and my secrets.

If there is something in these pages that inspires you to find a great deal, I will be happy. Conversely, I will not mind if you decide not to get into property. But I could not forgive myself if in ten years you said to me: "I *would* have got into property, only no one ever told me it was *this* good."

Successful investing!

Dolf de Roos
August 2004

PART ONE

Why Is Property So Good?

Chapter 1

FOUR MAGIC QUESTIONS

The purpose of this book is not so much to give you the "how-to" of real estate—although there will be plenty of how-to advice—but to make you sit bolt upright and exclaim: "Wow, I never realized real estate was this good!" The reason is that once you "get it," once you understand why property is such a phenomenally lucrative and astoundingly simple investment vehicle, you will never be able to focus on a sitcom on television again without getting itchy feet, wondering whether the hour wasted watching the tube is costing you the Deal of the Decade. You will be itching to apply my how-to ideas (and those gleaned from other books and sources), and you will also want to invent your own and go out there and try them, modify them, and continually improve them.

I will show you that contrary to expectations and what we somehow seem to have been taught by our parents, relatives, schools, the mass media, and "experts," it is possible to find a bargain property, or even many of them in a row. It is possible to buy properties using mostly *or entirely* other people's money. It is possible to buy properties where the returns are 20 or 30 or 50 or 100 percent or more per annum. What's more, all these things are easy.

When I tell people that property is not just as good as other investments, not just a little better, and not even just a lot better than other investments, but tens or even hundreds of times better than other investments, most people do not believe it.

So, let me in the next few pages show you why I think property is so much better.

Imagine you have a lump of money to invest. It does not matter whether you have $5,000, $10,000, $100,000, or $1 million, as the same principles apply in each case. So let's assume that you have $100,000 cash to invest. Let's also assume that you are considering investing your funds either in the stock market or in property. Finally, for the sake of simplicity, let's ignore all brokerage fees and commissions.

I will simply pose four questions . . .

Question One

How many dollars' worth of stock can you buy with $100,000 cash?

I often ask this question during seminars and am not infrequently met with a sea of blank faces, as if it were a trick question. It is not!

For most people, when you have $100,000 of cash to invest in the stock market, you can buy exactly $100,000 worth of stock.

Now I know some of you will protest that you can buy stocks on margin, but the reality is that investment houses will only let you do that with a very limited number of stocks, and then only for about 30 percent of the value of the stocks. What's more, if the stocks go down in value, they will make a "margin call," in other words, ordering you to pay a portion of the plummeted value so that your borrowing percentage is down to within their acceptable margins again. The truth is that for nearly all stock market investors, they put up the entire purchase price in cash.

So, in nearly all cases, your $100,000 cash will buy you exactly $100,000 worth of stock.

Let's compare this with investing in real estate.

How many dollars' worth of property can you buy with $100,000 cash?

Well, clearly, you could buy a $100,000 property. But you could also buy a $200,000 property, by taking out a mortgage for 50 percent of the property's purchase price. You could also buy a $300,000 property by taking out a 66 percent mortgage. In fact, you could buy a $1 million property by taking out a 90 percent mortgage.

Now I know that for many of you the notion of buying $1 million worth of property with a mere $100,000 cash is way beyond your comfort zone, and into the fear territory of your minds. The figure of $1 million may be a bit daunting, and then you can't help but think that if you have a $900,000 mortgage, how on earth are you going to pay the interest on that? After all, at a nominal 8 percent interest per annum, that would amount to $72,000 per year in interest, which may be more than you are presently earning!

The answer is that if you did buy a $1 million property with $100,000 cash, you would have an asset worth $1 million that would generate rental income for you. If you had bought wisely, then the rent would more than cover your expenses.

The point is that when you buy stocks, you generally have to put up the entire purchase price in cash. When you buy property, you generally have banks and other lending institutions falling over themselves to give you money.

People often challenge me on this claim that banks and financial institutions fall over themselves to lend you money to buy property. They often cite difficulties they have had with such institutions, and use examples of these difficulties to counter my argument.

They are totally missing the point. Anywhere in the world you can pick up a newspaper or magazine, look at television ads, or be confronted by huge billboards. You will never see advertisements saying things like: "Want to invest in diamonds, or antiques, or paintings, or precious metals, or stocks, or certificates of deposit (CDs), or mutual funds, or phone cards? Come and see us, and we will lend you the money to invest." It sounds crazy, right? Yet these same newspapers and magazines and television channels and billboards continually run advertisements offering financing for property acquisitions.

Remember how when you buy a new (for you, anyway) car, you suddenly notice all the other cars of the same make and model on the road? Well, when you look out for advertisements of institutions looking to lend you money to buy property, you will suddenly see them all over the place. And then you will also notice the lack of ads offering financing for other investments.

There is another way of looking at it. Imagine going into the bank, and saying to your bank manager something like: "I want to invest in gold, and my neighbor says that platinum is a good investment, and my kids are really into phone cards and baseball cards, and my husband (or wife) collects antiques, and we want to buy more stocks and bonds, so will you please, Mr. Bank Manager, lend us the money to invest in these things?" Chances are he will laugh you out of his office. And yet if you were to ask that same bank manager for money to buy property, he will look at the situation with interest, as he is generally eager to lend money on property.

This tells you two things about property. First, it is still considered a safe and secure investment. As further proof of this, consider the interest rates charged on various loans. The interest rate charged on real estate loans is less than that charged on business loans, which in turn is less than that typically charged on credit card balances. Clearly, banks exact higher interest rates where the perceived risk is higher.

Second, the important thing to note from the observation that bank managers happily lend money on property (but almost nothing else) is that when you acquire property, you don't even need most of the money required for the purchase! What a dream situation!

Think about this for a moment. Banks have the money (oodles of it!) but fortunately do not want to buy property (otherwise what would stop them from buying it all themselves?). And you want to buy property, but don't have (all of) the money. What a great opportunity for synergy!

This brings us full circle: With $100,000 cash, you can generally buy $100,000 worth of stocks, whereas that same $100,000 cash can buy you $1 million worth of property.

The advantage of this leverage is self-evident. If both stocks and properties went up by, say, 10 percent, then your stocks would have gone to $110,000 (a profit of $10,000), meaning that you would have made a 10 percent return on your invested capital. Your property would similarly have gone from $1 million to $1.1 million (a profit of $100,000), meaning that you would have made 100 percent return on your *invested* capital.

Of course leverage works in both directions. If everything goes down by 10 percent, then the stockholder would only lose 10 percent of his invested capital, whereas the property investor would lose all of it. However, I will show in the next chapter why I am not overly concerned with this risk of a downturn.

Question Two

The moment you buy your $100,000 worth of stock using your $100,000 cash, how much is your stock worth?

If Question 1 (from a few pages back) as it relates to stocks draws blank stares during seminars, Question 2 creates discomfort, as most people seem to assume that this time it must really be a trick question. Once more it is not!

By definition, at any point in time, a stock is worth that price at which willing buyers and willing sellers agree to transact a parcel of shares. Even though there may be many tens of thousands of existing stockholders who could be either potential sellers or buyers, and an even larger body of people who could be potential buyers, all of whom may have wildly varying ideas as to what the stock is worth, the market is structured so that at any given time, there is only one valid market price for that stock. Any and all transactions are effected at that one same price until, through the forces of supply and demand, the one price moves to a different level. In other words, at any one time, there is one, and only one, market price for that stock.

Thus, the moment you buy $100,000 worth of stock using your $100,000 cash, it is worth exactly $100,000.

The moment you buy your $1 million property using your $100,000 cash and a mortgage of $900,000, how much is your property worth?

Answers to this question tend to be somewhat guarded, but from an audience there is generally a muted consensus that the property is worth $1 million the moment you buy it.

Well, let me just toss some ideas your way. . . .

Is it not possible that the property for which you just paid $1 million using your $100,000 cash and a mortgage of $900,000 is only worth $650,000, and that some fast-talking owner or agent talked you into paying too much for it? Is it not possible that you bought a lemon?

Of course it is! It happens all the time. Just as people can pay too much for a used car, only to find out later that there is the proverbial sawdust (or banana skin) in the gear box, and just as you can talk yourself into believing that a painting is a steal because you think it is a Rembrandt, only to discover later that it truly was stolen, or that it was a bad copy and therefore not worth 10 percent of what you paid, so too can you pay too much for a property.

By the same token, is it not possible that the property for which you just paid $1 million using your $100,000 cash and a mortgage of $900,000 is worth $1.5 million, and that some slow-thinking owner or agent let you get away with paying too little for it? Is it not possible that you bought a phenomenal bargain?

Of course it is! It happens all the time. Just as people will sell you a car incredibly cheaply because "we are leaving town tomorrow and just want to cross it off our list," and just as you can get a painting for a song because the owners inherited it and never liked it in the first place and didn't think it was worth much, and you then find out it is a master after all, so too can you get a property for what seems like a steal.

It happens every day of the week. In fact, it is much easier to buy a bargain than a lemon for the simple reason that even if you sign a contract (subject to finance) to buy a lemon, the bank will not lend you money on it, as the appraisal will reflect its true value and not the contract price. Bingo! An instant and invisible lemon-avoidance algorithm.

Now I know from experience that when I say "It happens

all the time!" many people need more convincing. After all, they say, if it happens all the time, why has it never happened to me?

Well, the problem is that too many people think that if something sounds too good to be true, then it must be. If that is your belief, if that is what you have been brought up to think, then every time you come across something that sounds too good to be true (like a building worth $1.5 million that is on the market for $1 million), you will dismiss it as a hoax, as a con, or as a fiction of someone's imagination, and you will move on to more "believable" deals.

Therefore, you will limit yourself to deals of mediocrity, to the plain vanilla, ordinary, so-so deals with little upside potential that most of the rest of the world languishes with.

Does this mean that all deals that sound phenomenal are in fact phenomenal? Of course not! But dismissing them out of hand merely because they sound good definitely means limiting yourself to those horrid deals of mediocrity.

Even if you accept that phenomenal deals may exist, you may still be wondering why anyone in their right mind would sell a building worth $1.5 million for a mere $1 million. There are too many reasons to list here, but let me give you some examples. . . .

The most common reason why properties are sold at way below their true value is, unfortunately, divorce. When people are blissfully married they can reason lovingly and at length, but when things go awry, the battlers want instant results. So if it is agreed to sell a jointly owned home, the owners generally want each other out of their hair as soon as possible, and they therefore want their money out fast. There is no time to prepare the property for a good sale, and sometimes even no time to get an updated appraisal. Let's just sell the property NOW, split the proceeds, and never talk to each other again.

Not getting an appraisal is a surprisingly frequent reason why properties are sold at way below the market value. One example is when people are in a hurry, such as in a divorce situation as we have just seen. Other times, the owner may think he knows it all anyway, and since the house up the street sold for $360,000, and the house down the street sold for $345,000, he feels he is getting a good deal by selling his at $370,000, when in fact any of a dozen appraisers would have put a value of $480,000 on his property since his is the only one with a triple garage, a swimming pool, and a view to die for.

Sometimes the owners are simply too stingy to engage the services of an appraiser. They think that by saving the appraisal fee (typically around $500 for a single residence), they are putting that money in their pocket, when in actual fact they may be depriving themselves of many tens of thousands of dollars of potential sale price.

Perhaps the owners have lived in the house since 1957, when they bought the property for $3,200, and they now think they are ripping you off by accepting $285,000 for it, when in actual fact the property is genuinely worth $390,000.

Or a property may have been bequeathed to four children. One of them wants to live in it, the second wants to rent it out, the third wants to turn it into a commune, and the fourth is hiking in Nepal and cannot be contacted. General disharmony ensues, and in the end the lawyers (including the one with the power of attorney for the hiker) arrange to sell the property quickly and split the proceeds four ways.

Very commonly a property may be sold by people who have no vested interest in getting the true market value for it. This is often the case with foreclosure situations, where the bank is mainly interested in getting its mortgage back, but also occurs when people are asked to look after someone else's affairs. For instance, young Tommy may be asked to go back East to sell dearly departed Grandpa's house and small shopping mall, because no one else in the family can take the time off work. However, the reason Tommy doesn't have a job is because he likes partying, so back East he does not bother to do his homework to get the best price—he assigns the task to a randomly chosen real estate agent (a rookie with two weeks' experience), and both Tommy and the agent are ecstatic to get a sale price of $1 million, when the true value was, you guessed it, $1.5 million.

Each reason why people sell a property at well below its market value is unique, but they are there nonetheless. Believe it, and you will find them. Do not believe it, and you can join the masses who can say with complete honesty and accuracy that "that sort of thing never happens to me!"

So far, we have asked two of our four magic questions. We have seen that when you invest $100,000 in the stock market, you get exactly $100,000 worth of stocks that are worth exactly $100,000 the moment you buy them. Conversely, when you invest $100,000 in property, you can buy $1.5 million worth of property for a contracted price of $1 million using a $900,000 mortgage. Let's move on to the third question.

Question Three

When you buy your $100,000 worth of stock for a purchase price of $100,000 (and the moment you buy it, it is in fact worth exactly $100,000), what can you personally do to increase the value of your stock portfolio?

"Pray!" I hear you say. How about writing a letter to the directors of the company wishing them well? Or how about going out and buying as much and as many of the products or services that the company provides as you can afford?

I think you will agree that your options are limited.

When you buy your $1.5 million property for a contract price of $1 million using your $100,000 cash and a mortgage of $900,000, what can you personally do to increase the value of your property?

Wow! Where do we start?

You could paint the property. If you do not believe that it is possible to buy a property for $60,000, have it painted, and then sell it for $80,000, then you are missing out on spectacular opportunities.

Wait a minute, you say, let's slow up a bit! Why would anyone be willing to pay $80,000 for a painted house, but not $60,000 for one in dire need of a $400 paint job?

The answer lies in the way we have been conditioned to expect instant results. We want, expect, and can generally get instant soup, instant coffee, instant passport photos, instant credit card application approvals, instant messaging, Jiffy Lubes, and Curry in a Hurry. So when the masses go looking at properties, and they see an old house with bare wood exposed on the siding, they tend to dismiss it as being a rotten old property that will require a lot of work and effort (it probably has many things wrong with it besides the condition of the paint)—definitely no instant gratification! Most people would rather rot in front of the television set than pick up a paintbrush and paint a $20,000 profit for themselves in a couple of days (or better yet, pay someone to paint it for them for a modest $10, $20, or, who cares, even $50 an hour while they spend the time saved looking for the next $20,000 profit).

Magically, when that same house is painted, the masses will see it as a cute cottage in excellent condition that they could move into instantly, that would be a delight to live in, and that they could (instantly!) show off to their friends. Perception is reality!

Well, so much for our first idea on how you could increase the value of your investment in property. There are many other ideas . . . You may increase the value of your property by replacing the rusted gutters and downspouts on the front, by putting in a new heating/cooling system, by changing the curtains or drapes, by modernizing the bathroom, by putting in a new kitchen, by painting the roof, by erecting or replacing a fence, by installing an alarm system, by fitting new doorknobs throughout, by changing the window shades, by adding a swimming pool, by removing an old shed, by cleaning the carpets, or by paving the driveway.

On commercial properties you can increase the value by finding a tenant for a vacant space, by splitting a large area that may be worth only $5 per square foot and for which you have no tenants into two smaller areas worth $7 per square foot and for which you can easily get tenants, by (again) painting it, by agreeing to a longer lease length, by attracting a better tenant, or by replacing the carpets.

There are literally 101 things you can do to massively increase the value of your property without spending much money. In fact, to prove it, I have written a book detailing just that (see Appendix). We will explore some of these ideas in more detail later in this book.

But for now, let's get back to the point. Whereas with most other investments there is little you can do to increase the value of the investment, with property you are only limited by your imagination.

This brings us to our fourth and final question for this section . . .

Part of the reason why we invest is in the anticipation that things will go up in value. So, let's assume that all invested assets have doubled in value. (I am not specifying a time frame here—it may happen in a year or over a period of many years.) That means that the $100,000 stock portfolio has doubled to $200,000, and that the $1.5 million property has doubled to $3 million.

Question Four

You bought $100,000 worth of stock with $100,000 cash that was worth $100,000 the moment you bought it. It has doubled in value to $200,000. What must you do to enjoy some of the increased value?

Well, for most investors, the simple answer is: "Sell!" You could sell the entire portfolio, and thereby get your original $100,000 investment back plus $100,000 profit, or you could sell a portion of it. Either way, depending on the tax jurisdiction you are in, you will be up for capital gains tax, which will take some of the wind out of your windfall. What's more, by selling part of the portfolio, you are reducing the amount that is left that can earn further profits for you. Something sounds counterproductive!

You bought $1.5 million worth of property for a contract price of $1 million using $100,000 cash and a mortgage of $900,000. It has doubled in value to $3 million. What must you do to enjoy some of the profit?

By now you have probably learned to expect something other than the pat answer: "Sell it!" And you'd be right. Selling the property would be the dumbest thing you could do! Why sell it? After all, you own an asset, the value of which is indexed for inflation. It is generating a passive rental income that is similarly indexed for inflation. As time goes on, both the value of the property and the income it generates will continue to creep up. What's more, if you were silly enough to sell, you may have to pay capital gains tax on the profit.

But, I can hear some of you say, if you don't sell, how will you ever access the increase in value?

The answer is simply to refinance. You get a new appraisal (this time for $3 million) and go back to the bank and ask for a new mortgage. At the 90 percent loan-value ratio, you would get $2.7 million in your hands. After paying off the original $900,000 mortgage, you would still have $1.8 million left over of surplus new cash in your hands.

And ask yourself this question: Is the $1.8 million taxable? Of course not! Why would it be taxable? It is not income, so there would be no income tax due. Similarly, you have not sold the property, so there can be no talk of a capital gains tax.

You could use this $1.8 million as a 10 percent deposit on a further $18 million worth of property, which, combined with the $3 million you already own, makes your total portfolio worth $21 million.

At this stage, if property values were to go up a mere 1 percent, you would have made $210,000 (1 percent of $21 million). And the surplus passive rental income cash flow would be very handsome. If the property were to go up by 10 percent (perhaps in one year, or perhaps over a period of, say, five years), then you would have made a further $2.1 million (10 percent of $21 million). At this stage you could again refinance, pull some more money out, and invest in more property, or you could buy anything else such as an airplane (tax-deductible if you use it to fly around inspecting your expanding empire).

This airplane raises an interesting point. . . . As a broad generalization, the poor typically earn their money, pay their tax on it, and then spend what's left on the things they want. On the other hand, the rich earn money, spend it on the things they want, and then pay tax on what is left. Well, the property investor has an added benefit: When he refinances a property, first he receives money for which he has expended no effort (as in exchanging time for money); then, there are no tax obligations attached. Next, he gets to use this tax-free money to buy the things he wants (in this example an airplane). Furthermore, he gets a tax benefit from the interest payment on the money that he didn't even have to earn but simply got from the bank. Finally, he can *depreciate* the asset to give a further tax benefit. All aboard, please!

But I am getting ahead of myself.

My aim in writing this chapter is to share with you why I think property is not just *as good as* other investments, not just *a little bit better than* other investments, and not even just *much better than* other investments, but *tens and even hundreds of times better than* other investments.

My belief is that whereas most other investments do not offer significant leverage, property offers tremendous leverage through the generous application of mortgage financing. What's more, unlike with other investments, you can often buy properties at prices significantly below their true value, you can do things to them to further increase their value way beyond the cost of the improvement, and you do not need to sell to reap huge benefits from the increase in value.

Taken one at a time, the advantages just mentioned make real estate a phenomenally powerful investment vehicle. However, when considered in unison, when these advantages work together, the effects compound each other, and, as we have seen, an investment of a mere $100,000 may give you access to

$18 million without much effort at all. Even if it were only half as good, the resulting $9 million would still be phenomenal! Even if it were only one tenth as good, the $1.8 million would still be spectacular! Even if it were only one hundredth as good ($180,000), that is still, in my biased view, wildly better than the results of investing the same original starting capital of $100,000 in something that does not offer the advantages discussed in this chapter.

Now I have no illusions: For every argument and example I present in this book, there will be scores of detractors who will cry foul. They will seize specific clauses, phrases, sentences, and passages, and quote them in such a way to try to convince themselves or their audience that what I am saying cannot be right. They will say things like: "Where I come from you certainly cannot get 90 percent mortgages!" or "You cannot make $20,000 profit by spending $400 on paint and throwing in a weekend of labor in my town! Deals like that don't exist here."

If you choose to agree with them, that is fine by me! I will address the doom-and-gloom merchants, naysayers, disbelievers, and detractors later in this book. For now, please accept that what I have described here is my reality.

My contention is that most detractors of property do not fairly compare property with other investments. Consciously or subconsciously, they distort the truth, and then end up believing this distorted perception themselves. So, it is time to explore the benchmark used to compare most investments. You can then decide for yourself what is accurate and what is not.

Chapter 2

CONSPIRACY THEORY

There are two fundamental ways that the mass media, in my humble opinion, misrepresent how good real estate is. The first relates to how the media compare increases in house prices with increases in the values of other assets.

Increases in Asset Values

On Wednesday, December 27, 2000, a headline in *USA Today* read, "Housing Market Beats Stocks in 2000."

The first paragraph read: "When the numbers are in, 2000 will go down as one of those rare years in which Americans count their houses, not stocks, as their best-performing assets."

A table in the article, reproduced here, details how the value of various assets changed during the year.

Homes Beat Stocks in Value
The average value of a home increased more this year than many investments.

Home	7%
1-year CD	4.97%
Money market fund	5.5%
Dow Jones Industrials	−6.9%
Nasdaq composite	−39.6%

These results are appalling! Not because the statistics show that housing outperformed most other forms of investment, but the notion that in other years property trailed behind! A *rare* year? Get out of here!

The media's inability to grasp what I consider to be a fundamental advantage of investing in real estate is, I am sure, one of the prime reasons why potential investors, goaded on by financial advisors who have not yet figured out a way to profit from advising clients into property, stay away from property.

In any comparison, it is important to compare the proverbial apples with apples. Thus, in comparing the investment performance of your money invested in various sectors, it is important to always consider how the asset performed in relation to the *capital put in*. When you buy a CD—certificate of deposit—you have to put up the face value of the CD. As we have already seen, when you invest in the stock market (or money market funds), nearly all investors have to put up all of the cash representing the investment.

On the other hand, when you buy a property, you may choose to pay the full price in cash, but you can also (very easily!) get a mortgage for 20 percent, 50 percent, or 70 percent, of the value. There are mortgages available for 90 percent *and more* of the purchase price. In other words, it is not comparing apples with apples to compare the performance of a $100,000 investment in CDs, money market funds, or the stock market with a $100,000 property. And yet this is what most market commentators will do, and certainly what a lot of financial advisors do to convince their clients that property really is not that great.

What we should do is compare the performance of a $100,000 investment in CDs, money market funds, or the stock market with $100,000 invested *in* property. Thus, if this $100,000 was used as a 10 percent deposit on a $1 million property, then a 7 percent increase in property values would translate to an increase of $70,000 on our $1 million property, which is an increase of 70 percent on our original $100,000 investment in real estate.

Once again we have come up against leverage, or gearing. The same would apply to leverage in other forms of investment, but like it or not, banks and financial institutions love lending money secured against property, and shy away from lending money secured against nearly all other assets. In other words, gearing is readily available to property investors, and rarely available to investors in other asset classes.

So, if we can show that statistically most property investors are geared, while most money market and stock investors are not geared, then I believe it would be perfectly fair to compare the performance of property relative to other investments by taking this phenomenal power of leverage into account.

Calculated this way, even if the stock market goes up by 15 percent, and real estate goes up by only 5 percent, then any property investors with a modest mortgage of 70 percent would still have done better than their property-averse counterparts.

Since the average level of gearing on property in most Western nations fluctuates around 50 percent, is it not more accurate to show the percentage increases in house prices relative to invested capital, rather than property value? That would immediately double the returns for real estate!

Of course leverage also works in the other direction: If the market goes down, then the downside is amplified just as surely as the upside. But that brings me to a very interesting observation. . . .

Consider all the properties you have ever owned. And then consider all the properties your relatives and friends have ever owned. Have you ever known one to plummet in value by 60 percent, 90 percent, or even disappear off your balance sheet entirely?

That is exactly what happens to stocks and shares traded on markets around the world. In other words, a stock market may have an increase of, say, 5 percent in a year, but that really represents the average of many wildly disparate stock gyrations, with some going up phenomenally, others going under, and everything in between. Whether your collection of stocks does well or not is, it seems to me, a bit of a gamble.

On the other hand, it is much easier to see which properties will go up in value: Trends are slower, less volatile, and with fewer deviations from the average. Thus, the city with the highest growth in any nation in a particular year is very likely to be at or near the top again the following year. In other words it is stupendously easy to beat the national average! (That's probably what investors of technology stocks thought when they were popular, to their eternal regret.) We will explore this concept of beating the averages later in this book.

There is one more aspect that the newspaper failed to mention. Not only did the value of the property rise by more than the other asset classes, but the home also provided accommodation for the family. If they didn't own that home, then they would have had to pay rent somewhere else. And rent on your own home is not tax-deductible, whereas mortgage interest in most countries is. Yet the table at the beginning of this chapter fails to take any of these factors into account.

Yields

The second way in which the performance of property is often misrepresented is when reference is made to the relative yields of various investments.

Just to clarify, the yield is, by definition, the ratio of the annual income generated by the investment, divided by the dollar amount of the investment.

A typical scenario is as follows. It is boldly claimed that while yields on properties averaged, say, 6 percent in a given year, the average yields on stocks averaged, say, 19 percent, so why would you be bothered with all the hassles of real estate investing when you can get a better return from something that requires much less involvement?

On the face of it this seems like a sensible argument, and I know from the countless people who have told me so in person, by phone, fax, e-mail, or letter, that such advice was an ongoing reason why they did not get into the real estate game at a much earlier stage.

To understand why such a comparison is nonsense, we have to, once again, compare apples with apples.

When you invest $100,000 cash in the bank, and you receive $6,000 per annum in interest, then the yield is simply 6 percent. (The true yield will vary somewhat depending on whether the interest is paid monthly, quarterly, annually, or even weekly, daily, or continuously, and whether it is paid in arrears or in advance. However, in all cases it will be close to 6 percent, so let us just generalize and agree that the yield is 6 percent.)

Similarly, when you buy a property for $100,000 and you receive $6,000 per annum in rent, then the yield is, by definition, 6 percent. (Again, technically there will be a difference depending on whether the rent is paid weekly, biweekly, monthly, quarterly, or annually, but let's again generalize and agree that the yield is 6 percent.)

On the basis of yield alone, it would be fair to say that both investments returned the same amount.

Many advisors who are property-averse are quick to quote the relatively low yields of real estate, and go on to steer their clients into other investment arenas.

However, is that where the comparisons should end? By now you should be jumping out of your skin saying, "What about leverage?"

Whereas the $100,000 deposit in the bank required $100,000 in cash, the $100,000 property could be bought, using our 90 percent loan-to-value ratio, using only $10,000 cash. So the rental return of $6,000 should be considered relative to the cash input, not the arbitrary purchase price.

Of course, if we do that, then we have to take the interest payments into account. If the interest rate is, say, 5 percent, then we would be paying $4,500 in interest, and we would be left with $1,500 per annum ($6,000 in rent collected minus the $4,500 mortgage interest payments). Done that way, the return would be 15 percent ($1,500 divided by the $10,000 cash input).

As the owner of the property you also have property taxes, insurance, maintenance, pest control, management fees, and a variety of other expenses that have to be taken into account.

Then again, on the plus side, for taxation purposes, you can depreciate the building, usually at around 2.5 percent to 4 percent depending on where you live. Furthermore, the contents of the house—the chattels, or fixtures, or fittings, whatever you want to collectively call the lamp shades, curtains, drapes, vertical blinds, extractor fan, dishwasher, stove, fridge, washing machine, dryer, floor coverings, irrigation system, wiring, plumbing, and so on—can usually be depreciated at a much higher rate, typically around 20 percent to 30 percent. Note that depreciation means you can reduce your income for taxation purposes without it costing you even one cent out of your pocket of the amount depreciated.

Finally, when you deposit $100,000 in the bank for a year, then all you expect to get out of it is the interest. If you know what the interest rate is going to be, then you also know what the return on your investment will have been: It is only the $6,000 of interest earned, divided by the amount of the investment. This is really stating the obvious!

Conversely, when you buy a $100,000 property, at the end of the year its value may have changed. To know what return you have had on your investment, you will not only need to know all the cash flows into and out of the property (such as rent, maintenance, mortgage interest, and tax benefits), but you will also need to know how much the property will have changed in value during the year.

You may have noticed a subtle issue with the two situations above. When comparing the increases in asset values, the *USA Today* article compared the average rise in property values with the average returns from CDs and other cash investments. Other charts compare the cash flow yields of equity investments with the cash flow yields of properties. Apart from stocks, most financial instruments only enjoy either an income, or a capital growth, whereas property enjoys both.

Clearly, working out the true return on a property investment is much more complex than simply declaring the yield on a bank deposit. Later on I will explain how you can quickly and easily work out the true return on a property, and I promise you, this will be a real eye-opener, one that will make you say something like: "Why did no one ever explain it this way to me before?"

By buying into the notion that it is fair to directly compare property yields with the yields on other assets, or increases in property values with the increases in value of other assets, you may be missing out on some of the most lucrative investment propositions out there. *Always* compare apples with apples!

Chapter 3

A TAXING ISSUE

The tax laws as they relate to property are so incredibly diverse from one part of the world to the next, and so complex within each country, that it would really go beyond the scope of this book to attempt to give the reader specific tax advice as it relates to property investments in specific geographic locations. However, there are almost universally applied tax principles throughout the Western world that make investing in property even more lucrative than the previous chapters would suggest on their own.

For example, consider a property that has positive cash flow before tax. This means that before taxation is taken into account, your income exceeds your expenses, so that there is money left over. In the normal course of business, you would expect this profit to be taxed.

Imagine if I told you that, under certain circumstances, the tax man considers you to be running this property at a loss, and therefore lets you claim this "loss" against other income (even though you have positive cash flow!). The net effect of course is to increase your profits even more. Despite the fact that you are already making a profit before tax, the government boosts this profit so that after tax you are making even more.

It sounds too good to be true, right? And yet this is exactly what happens with property. (Once again I do not know of any other investment vehicle where you can easily and consistently have the government give you money even when you make a profit—rather than take it away in taxation.)

To understand why the government would boost your profits rather than tax you, you need to understand the concept of depreciation. In the normal course of events, assets used in business go down in value over time as they wear out, or as they are made obsolete through new technology. Governments want you to stay competitive and efficient, so they want to encourage you to upgrade your assets often. One incentive they give you is to allow you to depreciate your assets. As the assets go down in value, you can claim the decrease in value, or depreciation, against your income.

For instance, let's assume that you purchase a computer worth $10,000. We all know that computers go down in value quickly. In some countries you can claim 40 percent depreciation per year. This means that in the first year, you can claim $4,000 against your income as a write-off.

Now it hasn't really cost you $4,000 in cash during the year (you paid for the computer when you bought it) but the depreciation allowance is fair in the sense that in all probability the computer has indeed gone down in value.

Let's say that at the end of the year you want to sell the computer. Remember that you have claimed $4,000 in depreciation, so that the computer now has a "written-down book value" of only $6,000. If you only manage to get $5,000 for it ($1,000 less than the book value), then for tax purposes you can claim another $1,000 as a tax-deductible expense. Conversely, if you manage to sell it for $7,000, then you have to pay "depreciation recapture tax" (also known as depreciation recovered tax) on the $1,000 surplus of sale price over book value.

If you think it is fair to allow businesses to depreciate assets used to generate income, then the depreciation rules on a computer will seem sensible. In a similar manner, governments allow you to depreciate cars, trucks, fax machines, office furniture, and just about any other income-generating assets.

Now, computers, cars, trucks, fax machines, and office furniture do all go down in value. Property, on the other hand, as we will see in the next chapter, tends to go up in value. And yet the government allows you to claim a depreciation allowance on property. Are they silly enough to think that properties actually go down in value?

Of course not! They are well aware that there is a housing need, and furthermore that they are not efficient providers of housing for the needy. Therefore, by encouraging people like you and me to invest in property, they will not have to provide as many properties themselves for the needy.

Some of the depreciation you claim will represent items that truly go down in value by the amount of depreciation claimed. This may apply to curtains or carpets. But by the same token, you can depreciate not only the fittings, fixtures, and chattels in a house, but also the house itself (everything but the land—the government is not so silly as to assume that land goes down in value).

So we have this anomaly where you can claim depreciation on a property year after year, even though it may consistently be going up in value.

It is crucial to remember that when you claim depreciation, *it does not cost you any money.* So let's put some numbers to it. Imagine you own a property that is generating $20,000 per year in rent. Your expenses (mortgage interest, maintenance, property taxes, and so on) amount to $15,000. That leaves you with a pretax profit of $5,000. Normally you would expect to pay tax on the $5,000. However, if you had legitimate depreciation allowances of, say, $9,000, then your net income after deducting depreciation would be *negative* $4,000. In other words, you are in reality making a pretax profit of $5,000, but as far as the tax man is concerned, you are making a *loss* (on paper, anyway) of

$4,000. When this loss is applied against other income, you will effectively pay tax on $4,000 less than you would have if you did not own this property. At a marginal tax rate of, say, 40 percent, this will save you $1,600 in tax.

Effectively, the government has given you a check for $1,600, even though you were already making a profit before tax of $5,000. Thus, while your pretax income from the property is $5,000, your after-tax income is in fact $6,600, or 32 percent *more*.

Of course if your rental income is so high that your depreciation does not wipe out the profits (for tax purposes), then that is fine too! Making a profit is good.

If these hypothetical figures related to a $200,000 property, for which we paid a 10 percent deposit and for which we therefore got a 90 percent mortgage, then we could already conclude as follows:

The yield (the ratio of rental income to purchase price) is 10 percent ($20,000/$200,000).

The pretax cash-on-cash return is 25 percent ($5,000 income divided by $20,000 cash investment).

The after-tax cash-on-cash return is 33 percent ($5,000 + $1,600 divided by $20,000).

Notice how the boost to your cash-on-cash return from 25 percent to 33 percent by considering the benefits of depreciation is not reflected in the yield. This is why I said in Chapter 2 that the yield is not a good indicator of the performance of a property.

Now in some countries, there is a limit to how many losses (paper losses or real losses) in real estate you can offset against earned income. In the U.S. at present, that limit is set at $25,000 per year and decreases as your income goes above $100,000. However, in other countries there is no such limit at all. Thus, knowing the local tax laws can help you fine-tune your strategy for investing in that particular country.

Never underestimate the benefits of depreciation in property! In fact, one of the wisest investments you can make when you buy a property is to have an appraiser or registered valuer go through the property and itemize each and every chattel, fixture, and fitting in the property. Everything. The curtains, venetian blinds, vertical blinds, thermal drapes, the light fittings, carpets, rugs, suspended ceilings, refrigerator, garbage disposal unit, microwave oven, wall oven, stove, hot water heater, heating plant, air conditioner, pool pump, spa filter, and so on. You can even depreciate the wiring and plumbing in most jurisdictions! Whatever the fee charged by the appraiser, you will get that back many times over in the years to come in the form of higher depreciation write-offs.

The specifics of taxation as they relate to property investment in any one jurisdiction can fill an entire book. Always seek professional advice on how to deal with the taxes wherever you invest. The time and money spent seeking expert help will be repaid many times over in terms of tax saved or refunded.

Property is very tax-friendly. With which other investment vehicle can you be making a profit, and then still get more money from the tax man because he wants to encourage you?

Chapter 4

BEATING THE AVERAGES EASILY

*Statistics are just a group of
numbers looking for an argument.*

S
o far we have looked at how people evaluate property relative to other investments. We have talked about *averages* as if we all agree that averages are a fair and consistent measure that makes the comparisons watertight and convincing. Nothing could be further from the truth!

If we were out hiking, and I asked you whether you were warm or cold, and you replied that your feet were a little warm because you had thick shoes and socks on, but you had forgotten your hat and therefore your head was a bit cool, but that on average you were fine, then no one would try to take remedial action.

However, if I put one of your feet in a bucket of ice, and the other one in a bucket of boiling water, and told you that on average you must be about right, you would have a problem with me.

It is not enough to just consider the average! In both cases the average was about the same, but the variations from the average were not always acceptable.

The average payout on a lottery ticket is typically less than 30 cents on the dollar (after the organizers—often the state— get their share, along with the tax man, and the printers for printing the tickets, and the drivers who deliver them, and so forth). Based on the average payout of, say, $3 for a $10 ticket, no one in their right mind would ever buy one! Even if you bought all the tickets in a lottery and therefore were guaranteed to win every prize, you would only get a fraction of your investment back. On average, the returns are hopeless—you would be going backward! Yet countless gamblers buy tickets all the time.

It is not the average return that excites lottery gamblers. It is the hope that one day they will defy the odds and be the one in sixteen million (or whatever) to win. The lure of instant wealth overrides their ability or desire to work on a plan with a greater average chance of success. In this case you are counting on a high deviation from the average.

Remember, for every lottery winner, there are literally millions and millions of hopefuls, who dutifully, week after week, rain or shine, go out and buy a lottery ticket, even though they have been doing it for years and never won anything. The lure of the big win is enormous.

Beyond considering averages, we have to ask ourselves, what is our chance, realistically, of achieving the average?

To determine that, we have to consider two aspects related to averages:

1. How much does the investment sector I am considering (e.g., stocks or futures or property) fluctuate around its average?

2. How much does each specific investment within a sector (e.g., a particular stock or futures contract or property) fluctuate around the sector average?

Let's start with the first question. I will explain it graphically . . .

Stocks are often quoted as having a certain average growth over the long term. Let's consider some of these growth statistics.

In the United States, the stock market grew *on average* by 6 percent since 1960. However, this growth was not, as mathematicians would say, linear and monotonic, meaning going up by the same amount each and every year. Rather, the graph looks very jagged: Some years it went up a lot, other years it went down a lot, and in other years it was flat. The following graph shows the performance of the U.S. stock market.

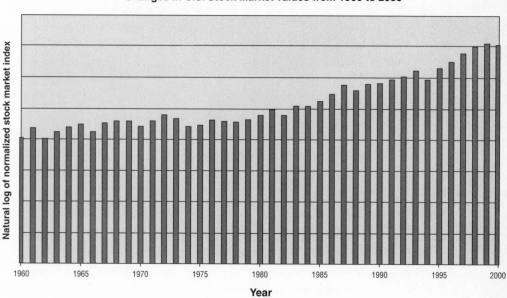

Changes in U.S. Stock Market Values from 1960 to 2000

By comparison, let's also look at how property values grew, *on average*, over the same period. The following graph shows the performance of property.

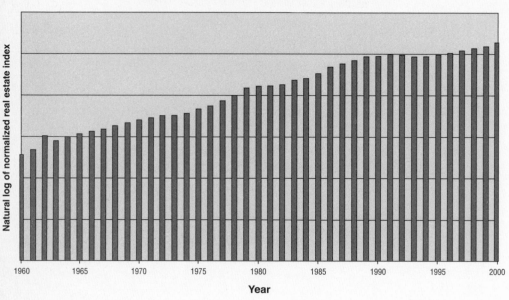

Changes in U.S. Real Estate Values from 1960 to 2000

As you can see, the growth in the stock market fluctuates far more wildly than the growth in the property market.

And this tends to be a universal trend. The preceding graphs relate to the United States. The results for Australia are shown in the following graph.

The numbers are different, and therefore the graphs are different, but the net effect is the same: The average increase in property values fluctuated far less than the average increase in the stock market.

What does all this mean for you, the investor?

It simply means that if you buy a property, the chance of that property going up in value by around the long-term national average is pretty high. The average increase is relatively consistent, smooth, predictable, and even boring!

Conversely, if you buy stocks, the chance of the stock mar-

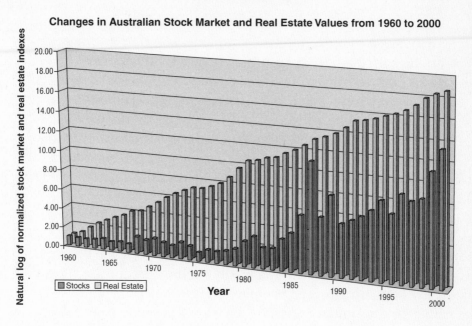

Changes in Australian Stock Market and Real Estate Values from 1960 to 2000

ket going up in value by around the long-term average is a bit of a gamble. In some years stocks may do much better than average. In other years they will do much worse than average. In many years, the average increase is negative!

But wait! It gets better (or worse, depending on what you have invested in).

Remember, the second question was "How much does each specific investment fluctuate around the sector average?"

In other words, if you buy a property at random, how will it fare relative to the national average increase of property values?

Please bear with me, for this is one of the most crucial points about real estate in this book.

If there are, say, 400 houses in a community, and 399 of them have increased in value by an average of, say, 5 percent, then the chances are extremely high that the 400th has also increased in value by around 5 percent. Property values tend to increase in unison for the simple reason that if someone is trying to sell a particular property at too high a price (higher than average), then buyers will forgo it in favor of another property whose price conforms more closely to the going market rate—the average.

Conversely, if there are 400 stocks listed on an exchange, and 399 of them have increased in value by an average of, say, 5 percent, then there really is no telling just how much the 400th may have increased in value.

In the case of the properties, the 399 not only averaged 5 percent, but each one individually increased by very close to 5 percent. In the case of the stocks, the 399 averaged 5 percent, but each one increased by a wildly varying amount: Some may have gone up by over 1,000 percent (the way Qualcomm did in 1999 in the United States, or the way PDL did in New Zealand in 1992), some may have gone under, and others may have sat on exactly 5 percent. In other words, knowing the average increase of stock values does not give us much of a clue as to how a particular stock will fare, whereas knowing the average increase in property values gives us a good idea as to how much a particular property—or any property—will fare.

Mathematically, we would say that the standard deviation is much less. The standard deviation of changes in property values is much smaller than the standard deviation of changes in stock values.

Granted, in some parts of the country, property prices increase faster than in others. (Indeed, this fact forms the basis of the single biggest reason why it is possible to do extremely well in property, as will be discussed shortly.)

For example, if the national increase in property values is 8 percent, then it is entirely possible that property prices increase on average by 10 percent in California, and only 5 percent in South Dakota. Furthermore, within California, prices in San Francisco may increase on average by 12 percent, and only by 8 percent in Eureka. And within San Francisco, prices may increase by 14 percent in the Presidio, and "only" 11 percent in Russian Hill. But whether you consider values nationwide, statewide, citywide, or suburb by suburb, these trends are extremely stable and therefore predictable. In other words, a house in the Presidio in San Francisco is very likely to increase in value by the same amount as other houses in that neighborhood.

So much so that when considering a property, most financiers, appraisers, bankers, and investors want to know the "comps"—the comparables to that property. In other words, how much are comparable properties (those in the same or similar neighborhoods with a similar number of bedrooms, bathrooms, and so forth) selling for? The values and trends of other properties will tell you what this one is likely to be doing.

Compare this with stocks. We have already seen that if stocks go up on average by 5 percent, then that gives us little clue as to what a particular stock may go up by. So now let's look at particular industry sectors (a loose analogy to the regions we discussed regarding properties).

Assume that the stock market has gone up by an average of 8 percent, technology stocks have gone up by 10 percent on average, and airline stocks by only 5 percent. If within technology stocks, those related to the Internet have gone up by 14 percent, what are the chances that the XYZ Corporation, which is an Internet company, will have gone up by 14 percent?

Who knows? There is no reason at all to assume that it will perform anywhere near or far from 14 percent.

There is so little correlation between the performance of one company on the stock market and another, between one company in a particular industry sector and another in that same industry sector, between one company in a specific market niche and another in that same niche, that in evaluating a company, you are never asked for the comps on a stock.

Put simply, house prices tend to go up in tandem with their peers, while stock values fluctuate tremendously with much more autonomy in relation to their peers.

Seen in this light, investing in the stock market has a much higher gambling element than investing in property.

You may counter this by saying that, using my arguments, if you invest in property, you cannot hope to do much better than average, whereas if you invest in stocks, you can easily do better (up to 1,000 percent in a year, as lucky investors in Qualcomm and PDL experienced).

True! But if it were that simple, then most stock market investors would beat the pants off property investors, and my studies tend to suggest the opposite.

First off, when you invest in anything other than property, you do not get the tremendous benefits discussed in Chapter 2, namely buying many dollars' worth of assets more than your available cash, being able to buy at well below market values, being able to increase the values way beyond expenditure, and not needing to sell to realize your profit.

Second, to do well (really well) in most investment areas, you need to develop specialist knowledge, for which a sophisticated vocabulary comes in handy. With property, common sense and just a handful of key words are adequate to make a fortune.

Sure, if you pick the right stock, then a dollar invested in that stock may well do much better than a dollar invested in property. However, if you take 1,000 stock investors at random, and plot their performance, and then you take 1,000 property investors at random, and plot their performance, then in the long run, and relative to cash invested, the property investors outperform the stock investors by a wide margin.

This is not entirely unexpected. Companies can be

formed and dissolved very quickly (and frequently are!). When a new technology comes along, a whole industry may be rendered obsolete. For instance, when calculators first appeared on the scene in the late 1960s, slide rules were made redundant. Similarly, the advent of fax machines rendered telex machines obsolete, while fax machines in their turn are being largely replaced by e-mail and the transfer of files over the Internet.

Property, on the other hand, is much slower to be replaced.

Sometimes, properties remain for centuries (which is one of the reasons why Europe is so endearing to visitors from the New World). Certainly most properties are around for many generations. Most people at some stage in their lives go back to where they were brought up. For most of us, when we visit the neighborhoods of our childhood, we marvel at how small the homes were that seemed so big when we were little. The point here is, nearly everyone's original homes are still around.

When I was a child, my family moved around a lot internationally. Of the dozen homes that at some stage we owned or rented in various countries, all but one were still standing on my most recent visits there (the one that was demolished, on the corner of Union and Fourth Streets in Dunedin, New Zealand, was requisitioned by the local city council to expand the university facilities). All the other homes are still there, and some of these date back to the 1950s and 1960s.

Compare that longevity with the fate of companies listed on the local stock market. Some big names have been around seemingly forever (IBM, Ford, Hertz, 3M, HP, and so on). But there are countless scores of companies from twenty years ago that young adults today have never heard of, because they simply are no longer around. Indeed, even many companies that everyone knows today weren't around twenty years ago, such as Handspring, Lucent, and AOL.

Companies come and go, but the buildings they work out of, and the homes that the workers live in, tend to stay around for a long time.

There are very few reasons why properties "disappear." Let's briefly consider the mechanisms by which you may "lose" a property: requisitions, earthquakes, landslides, fire, and re-development.

In the case of our family home in Dunedin, mentioned above, it was requisitioned by the city council. But do you think they just kicked us out and said: "Sorry, folks, this is now ours"? No way! They had to compensate us with a fair market value. Thus, even when you lose a property through government requisition (be it to widen a road, put in a highway, make a reservoir, or whatever), *you get compensated.*

Earthquakes are surprisingly prevalent—recall the massive earthquake of magnitude 7.9 on the Richter scale in India in early 2001. There have been, in recent history, devastating earthquakes in Kobe, Japan (1995), Turkey (1999), and Italy (1997). In the United States, nearly everyone remembers the San Francisco quake of 1989, and has learned of the far more devastating earthquake there of 1906. Were homes and commercial buildings destroyed as a result of these earthquakes? Sure they were. But we have to consider two factors . . .

Statistically, the chance of losing a property to an earthquake is incredibly small. What is more, you can significantly reduce your chances by not buying properties in known earthquake zones! New York, for instance, is built on some of the most stable land on the surface of the planet. San Francisco, on the other hand, is prone to earthquakes.

Next, even if your property is completely wiped out by an earthquake, does that mean that you will have lost everything? Well, no! It may come as a surprise, but most people have insurance to cover them in the unlikely (for most of us) event of an earthquake.

In some countries, this earthquake insurance is compulsory. In New Zealand, for instance, there was a compulsory levy to the archaic-sounding Earthquakes and War Damages Commission, which covered you in both of those unlikely events.

In California, one of the world's earthquake hotbeds, while earthquake insurance per se is not compulsory, it is mandatory for insurance companies to notify their policyholders that earthquake insurance is available.

Anyway, the whole point is that losing your property to a requisition or earthquake need not mean you have lost the entire investment.

Losing a home to a landslide is not a common event. Anyone who was in New Zealand in the 1970s remembers the spectacular landslide at Abbotsford, where a couple of dozen homes slid down a muddy slope after a particularly heavy rainfall. I also remember a house in Greymouth sliding off a ridge in the 1980s. There are two points to note: In both cases insurance was able to cover the unlikely events. And landslides are so rare that I can clearly remember examples from three decades ago!

The dangers of fire are well known, but once again it is easy (and common) to have insurance protection against fire.

The final major category of how properties are removed from the pool of available properties to invest in is when one building is torn down to be replaced by another. This is called redevelopment of the site. A building may have outlived its useful life, but more commonly, the geographic location lends itself more to a completely new type of activity, and hence the old building is torn down and replaced. For instance, there may be a row of fifteen houses that are all acquired by one person or entity, which are then torn down and replaced with a block of shops, or a movie theater, or even a parking lot. Or alternatively, a house may simply be torn down to be replaced by a more modern one.

Even in these circumstances, when old buildings are torn down, the owners do not lose everything! Whether they are doing the redevelopment themselves, or whether they have willingly sold to the developer, in both cases they have agreed to go into the deal. It will have been worth their while.

Why have I gone on about all the possible mechanisms by which properties are taken out of circulation?

Because even though the percentage of properties lost in the last century to requisitions, earthquakes, landslides, fire, and redevelopment is minuscule in comparison to the total number of properties out there, in nearly all cases the capital loss sustained by the owners was minimal.

Let's now go back and compare this with stocks that are no longer around.

The number of companies that no longer exist is *not* a minuscule proportion of all companies that were ever formed! It is estimated by better business bureaus and chambers of commerce all over the Western world that around 50 percent of all new companies fail within the first year, and that by the end of the fifth year, some 80 percent have failed.

And when a company goes under, the investors in that company lose their investment, save the fire-sale value of what little plant, stock, and equipment may remain.

Even solid, respected companies that have been around for generations sometimes go belly-up. Who in the United States would have thought that Montgomery Ward would have failed? Or Bond Corporation in Australia, or Equitycorp in New Zealand?

Companies go under all the time. It is so much a fact of life, it is so common and prevalent, that we may raise our eyebrows when we hear a particular company has gone into liquidation, or receivership, or voluntary chapter 11 bankruptcy, or chapter 13 bankruptcy, but a few days later we have forgotten about it. It happens so often that it's not as if a handful stand out because of the rarity factor.

What is more, try phoning your insurance broker and asking him what the premium would be to take out insurance against a company on the stock market going under. His response would be interesting.

Properties very rarely go under, and *even if they do*, you are automatically compensated, or you can usually and relatively cheaply take out insurance against it. (The premiums are so low because the risk to the insurance company is so low.)

Conversely, companies very often go under, and when they do there is nothing you can do about it. Even insurance companies will not insure you against this. The premiums would be astronomical, because the risk to the insurance companies would be enormous.

So, one of the reasons why stocks fluctuate about their average so much more than properties do is that new companies are being created all the time, while existing ones are collapsing all the time.

The reason why the value of any one particular stock may vary so wildly from the national average is that any one company may have unique attributes that set it dramatically apart from other companies. It may have the brand name, patent, license, rights, or secret formula to something that is highly in demand that competitors cannot get. Such is the case with Kodak (they own one of the most widely known brand names in the world), Coca-Cola (a secret recipe), and Rockwell (patents on high-tech chips). Having an advantage over your competitors is likely to make your stock rise faster than average.

However, just as your stock may rise faster than average, so may it fall faster than average. For instance, Hewlett-Packard's laser printers dealt a big blow to IBM's electronic typewriters. The sands of business are constantly shifting. And the trick is to try and figure out which companies are going to perform better than average, and which are going to perform worse than average.

Properties, on the other hand, vary much less about the national average than companies. A three-bedroom, two-bathroom house in a particular area is generally worth about as much as any other three-bedroom, two-bathroom house in that same area (although, as we have seen in Chapter 2, you may purchase it for less than its true market value). The same goes for commercial property.

About the only factor that sets one property apart from another similar one is the location. A prime location sells at a premium for obvious reasons of views or proximity to, say, downtown or a particular street. However, if you come back in twenty years' time (or look at values twenty or forty years ago), then those same properties selling at a premium because of their location will still in all probability sell at a premium because of their location. Once again, properties vary much less about their national and local averages than stocks.

The Numbers Game

Everyone loves beating the odds. Everyone likes to think they have a plan or a system whereby they can do just that. The reality is rather sad.

Consider gambling at casinos. It surprises and amuses me to see countless thousands of pathetic, puffy-eyed hopefuls robotically inserting coins and pulling at the one-armed bandits, playing the roulette wheel, or craps, or baccarat, or whatever. Just like the gamble of lottery tickets, casino games (with one notable exception) are permanently stacked in the favor of the casino.

As an example, take roulette. There are thirty-six numbers on a roulette wheel. Half of them are black, and half red; half are even, and half odd. If you bet a dollar on black, and a red number comes up, you lose your dollar; if a black number comes up, you get your dollar back, plus one more. If this was all there was to it, then you could expect to win half your bets (and make a dollar each time) and lose the other half (and lose a dollar each time). You would expect to come out even.

Of course this is not all there is to it! There would be nothing in it on average for the casinos, and therefore there would be no profit left to pay salaries, and rent, and electricity, and advertising, and directors' fees, and staff bonuses, and vacation pay, and insurance premiums, and on and on. So, in their wisdom, the casinos added another number to the wheel—a green zero. If the ball rolls into the green zero, then all bets placed are forfeited to the house. (To be exact, you can "buy insurance" against the ball falling on the green zero, in which case you get to keep all bets except the one placed on the green zero—the "insurance premium." However, if you did that thirty-seven times, then on average you could expect to lose the premium thirty-seven times, and win $36 once, so that you would still be $1 down.)

So, the way the game works is that, on average, for every thirty-seven spins of the wheel, it would fall on red eighteen times (resulting in you losing $18), it would fall on black eighteen times (resulting in you winning $18), and it would fall on green once (resulting in you losing $1). The net loss would be one dollar in thirty-seven gambled, or a 2.7 percent loss. This is fixed—there is nothing you can do to change these odds. (American casinos typically have two green zeros, making the odds 5.26 percent in their favor.)

Despite my contention that there is nothing you can do to change these odds, countless books have been written on doing just that. These books proclaim strategies for putting the odds in your favor.

For instance, one common roulette strategy is known as "doubling down." Every time you win, you revert to your standard bet of, say, $1. But if you should lose, then you double your bet. So, if you bet $1 and lose, you increase the size of the next bet to $2. If you lose again, you increase it to $4. If you lose one more time, you increase the bet to $8. Let's assume that at this stage you win. Then you would have lost $1 + $2 + $4, for a total loss of $7, but you would have won $8 (from your final $8 bet). At the end of each losing streak, you would be exactly $1 up.

Presented in this light, you would have to agree that so long as you doubled each bet until you won, and then reverted to the original bet amount, you would end each sequence with a win. You cannot lose!

If only life were so simple. The problem is that every now and then you will get a long sequence of losses. This presents two problems. One, all betting tables have "house limits," meaning you cannot bet more than a certain amount. For tables that accept $1 bets, this is typically $500. In other words, if you lost eight times in a row, and doubled your bet eight times from $1 to $2 to $4 to $8 to $16 to $32 to $64 to $128 to $256, then you had better win that round, because if you didn't, you couldn't double your bet again to maintain your strategy. You would lose and the casino would have $511 of your money. Two, even if there were no house limit, after a relatively small number of doublings, you would run out of money to place on the table.

Whatever your strategy is, you cannot change the odds. With roulette, you lose 2.7 percent of the time on average. Period. All you can hope to do is alter the ratio between the number of bets you place before you lose all your money, versus the amount of money you lose when you do lose.

If you take 1,000 people at random, then on average they will have lost 2.7 percent of the money they bet on the roulette wheel. Your personal ability to do better than that is not based on any strategy—it is simply a matter of luck.

With the stock market, advisors always promote various

strategies. Simple strategies are to invest in certain sectors (most noticeably of late, their advice was to invest in the technology sector). Other strategies are to do what is referred to as "dollar-cost averaging"—buying more of a stock whether the price has gone up or down.

However, just as I have yet to see a strategy that can beat the casinos in the long run, I have yet to see a strategy for investing in the stock market that can be shown to beat the average over the long term. Is there a mutual fund out there that has consistently outperformed the average?

I have personal experience of this: I had more than a million dollars at stake in the stock market in early October 1987. Not one of my team of advisors could tip me off, despite all their analysis tools, computer hookups, and industry buddies, that a crash was imminent. Not only did I lose a lot, but they did personally as well. One of my brokers was reduced to teaching remedial classes after school to earn extra money.

What would be a strategy today to beat the average performance of the stock market?

Well, I have a strategy to beat the average in the property market. It goes as follows. . . .

Beating the Averages through Geography

When the report in the *USA Today* article referred to an average increase in house prices of 7 percent, they meant exactly that. Consider all the houses in the country, add together all the increases in value, and work out the percentage change.

Now consider a dinky little town somewhere in the back of nowhere. It may be the township that serviced a long-abandoned oil well or a shut-down nuclear power station.

Surely it is possible that the properties in this town did not go up by the national average?

That means that somewhere else, a bunch of properties must have gone up by more than the national average in order for the average to be what it is.

So let's put some geographic locations to this. Now please accept that I do not want to embarrass, insult, or upset anyone living in any regions mentioned! But in the United States, California is known to have exceptionally high growth. No wonder: The climate is wonderful, there are many things to do, and it is a very desirable place to live. Not surprisingly, people move to California from many other parts of the country. Partially for that reason, the growth in demand is greater than the national average, and as a result, prices have grown faster than average. Predictions are that over the next thirty years, the population of California is going to double again. Therefore, chances are that growth in California will continue to be higher than the national average.

Conversely, in places like North Dakota, Wyoming, and Iowa, there is not the same growth—people simply do not have the same desire to flock there. Consequently, growth is likely to be less than the national average.

These trends are relatively stable and predictable.

In other words, if you want to beat the national average, all you have to do is invest in those regions that for years have exceeded the national average.

Now if you live in Cheyenne, Wyoming, you may find this advice discomforting. You may say: "What is wrong with Cheyenne?" And I would have to answer that having been there, there is nothing wrong with the place per se, but that as far as real estate is concerned, it is not exactly bustling: At least a third of the commercial space downtown is vacant, and the statistics on residential property show slow growth for a long time. So, even if you wanted to continue living there, why would you invest there, when you can jump on an airplane, fly to a region that has higher than average growth, and invest there?

People are perversely obsessed with investing in their own town or city or area, when sometimes it would make much more sense to invest elsewhere.

Look at it from another perspective. Imagine you have never been to New Zealand, but you wanted to invest in real estate there. Now Auckland, in the north of the North Island, is the biggest city in the country. It is not the capital, but it has over one million inhabitants out of the total population in the country of some 4 million people. What's more, the population growth in Auckland is twice the national average.

At the other end of the country, at the bottom of the South Island, you have the city of Invercargill. It is the southernmost city in the country, and is about as close to Antarctica as you can get while still being in the civilized world. It only just qualifies as a city, as the population is around 40,000. Houses are cheap in Invercargill! A three-bedroom house that in Auckland would sell for $450,000 sells in Invercargill for a mere $75,000. In fact, many Aucklanders sell up in Auckland, take the proceeds of the sale of their house, buy an equal (or even better) house in Invercargill, invest the huge difference, and then spend the investment income paying the heating bill.

I'm only kidding about the heating bill, although it is a lot colder there than in Auckland. So far, you may think that Invercargill doesn't sound like such a bad place to live. But let me give you some more details. . . .

Between two censuses in the 1990s, which in New Zealand are conducted every five years, the population of Invercargill *declined* by 6 percent. What do you think the effect of that was on the property market?

With a shrinking pool of potential tenants and owner-occupiers, both capital values and rentals declined.

So why would you invest there instead of in Auckland?

In Australia, there is a lot of internal migration to the sunshine state of Queensland. The reasons are diverse—the climate is better than in other parts of the country, there are many things to do (most of the nation's amusement parks are there), the job growth is there, people like to go there to retire, and so on. In fact, the reasons are similar to why in the United States there has been a lot of internal migration to California.

By contrast, consider the island state of Tasmania at the southern end of Australia. It is spectacularly beautiful. Indeed, if you go to the capital, Hobart, which is itself very charming, and make your way up to the top of nearby Mount Wellington, the views are breathtakingly beautiful. But would I invest there?

Not by preference!

Despite the sheer geographic beauty of Tasmania, many people opt for the warmer climate further north—especially in Queensland. As a result, just like with Invercargill in New Zealand, the population growth has not only been lower than the national average, but it has at times been negative. Properties have ended up vacant, rental levels have come down, capital values have shrunk, and so the cycle of decline continues. In the last decade, three of the five major industries in Tasmania have closed down.

But here is the point. With the stock market, no one can predict with any degree of certainty which sectors will do well in the next five or ten years, and which will perform poorly. Consequently, it is very difficult to predict with any degree of certainty that a particular strategy will, in all probability, beat the market average. You have to wait and see. As such, the strategy is somewhat of a gamble.

On the other hand, with real estate, it is relatively easy to predict which geographic locations will do well. You do not even have to live in the country you are considering investing in. As we have seen, in the United States, the population of California is predicted to double in the next thirty years (California has already surpassed France as the world's sixth largest economy). Growth in California has exceeded the national average for a long time, and chances are it will continue to do so.

In New Zealand, Auckland has outperformed Invercargill for a long time, and chances are it will continue to do so.

In Australia, Queensland has outperformed Tasmania for a long time, and chances are it will continue to do so.

Indeed, within California, there are areas that consistently do better than the state average. San Francisco and Marin County have regularly had growth rates in capital values higher than the rest of the state. Similarly, in Queensland, the southeastern corner encompassing the Gold Coast, Brisbane, and the Sunshine Coast has regularly outperformed the rest of the state by a factor of two. Since Queensland is already growing at double the national average, by focusing your investment activity on the southeastern corner, you can reasonably expect to get a growth rate significantly higher than the national average.

Now it's probably time for a few disclaimers! I am not saying that investors in North Dakota, Invercargill, or Tasmania will always do poorly. On the contrary, if enough people shy away from these places, then that in itself will present golden opportunities. After all, these regions will still need hospitals, shops, banks, and homes for the people who choose to stay there. However, your chances of beating the national average are much greater if you focus on those geographic regions where it can be shown, statistically and definitively, that growth is consistently and sustainably higher than the national average.

Beating the Averages through Demographics

So much for beating national averages by choosing geographic locations that have higher than average growth.

What about property sectors that have higher than average growth?

Everyone knows that the baby boomers, those people born between 1946 and 1964, are entering retirement. Before long, many of them will be in need of retirement homes and assisted-living facilities. Even if the total population numbers do not change over the next fifty years, the proportion of elderly people will go up dramatically. Already the demand for rest home facilities in the Western world is increasing rapidly. The demand for leisure activities and all related services can also be expected to increase.

Given there is this predictable and inevitable trend toward an aging population, is there a reason why you would not invest to cater to the need?

In fact, the population in our well picked on North Dakota, Invercargill, and Tasmania is also aging. Therefore, if you wanted to invest in these regions, then catering to the elderly may easily enable you to beat the averages there. But that raises the following thought.

What if you were invest in those geographic areas where there is greater than average growth (say, three or four times the national average) and, furthermore, in those sectors that were also experiencing greater than normal growth (such as rest homes). Could you not reasonably expect your returns to be far greater than the national average?

Life Is a Holiday by the Seaside

As a final example of how to easily beat the national average in property (before I force you to think of some examples yourself), I ask you to think about why people live where they do.

A hundred years ago, in 1900, the Western world was essentially an agrarian society. In the United States, for instance, a significant proportion of the population worked on the land, producing 80 percent of the food consumed (the deficit was imported from abroad). By the year 2000, only 4 percent of the population worked on the land, producing more than 120 percent of the food consumed (the surplus is now exported).

The change that permitted a mass exodus from the land (rural living) to cities (urban living) was mechanization and automation. A tractor could plow as much in a day as 100 men with oxen or horses. Refrigerated trucks and ships enabled the transportation of food to new markets where previously that food would have spoiled en route. Crop-duster airplanes for aerial spraying and fertilizing could achieve in an hour what would have taken a week 100 years ago.

Every operation became much more efficient, eliminating the time-consuming human component. The people no longer required to work the land were not relegated to the unemployment heap, however. On the contrary, vast armies of workers were required to design, prototype, commercialize, manufacture, assemble, test, deliver, install, service, and maintain millions of tractors, trucks, and airplanes, to name but a few of the manufactured goods that typified the move away from an agrarian society.

And so there was a slow but consistent shift in populations away from the rural sector to cities where manufacturing was concentrated. Some cities were so dominated by one or two main industries that they are still associated with that industry, such as Detroit with cars, Pittsburgh with steel, Hollywood with movies, Blackpool with coal, Mt. Isa with mining, Zurich with finance, and Milan with fashion.

Note that people didn't just drift from the land to end up congregating in these places, and then spontaneously decided to start an industry there, such as making cars in Detroit.

Rather, the (initially) nascent industries attracted workers from the land as employment opportunities rose in the new industries while they fell on the land.

In other words, part of the reason why cities grew the way they did in the twentieth century was that the dominant industries were hungry for more and more workers, who had to live near their place of employment.

However, the world is changing once again. All the industries that required armies of workers during the last century are themselves being automated and mechanized. Assembly plants now exist that are entirely run by robots. Financial trading houses that once had hundreds of brokers running around and interacting with scraps of paper, shouts, hand signals, and other cues, now are entirely computerized. Movies have been produced entirely inside computers, and trains exist that are fully automated and do not even have a driver.

In addition to this phenomenal wave of automation, communications technology (epitomized by the Internet) has permitted both incredible mobility (you can call the office on your cell phone while driving to the ski slopes) and an incredible stay-at-home power (you can video-conference for two hours with co-workers from around the world instead of all but one having to spend two days traveling to meet one another).

And here is the point. The reason why people came together to live in big, sprawling cities (which, as a result, became overcrowded, polluted, crime-infested, and short on resources such as water and open space) has disappeared. No longer do the masses need to live on each other's doorsteps, so to speak. No longer do we have to congregate within an easy commute of our places of work. For an increasing proportion of the population, through the judicious use of communications technology, we have the freedom to live where we want.

Just hold this thought, for a moment: We have the freedom to live where we want.

And now go back to your childhood, and try to think of where everyone wanted to go for their summer vacations. Nine out of ten friends and acquaintances that I have asked this question answer: "To the beach!" or "To the seaside!" All the holiday resorts from my memory were at the beach: Schreveningen in Holland, Kortrijk-aan-Zee in Belgium, St. Tropez in France, Brighton in England, Whangamata and Sumner in New Zealand, and the Gold Coast in Australia.

The allure of the seaside is varied and deep-seated. For a start, the scenery is usually far more interesting—and certainly more alive—than at inland locations. Sunrises or sunsets over water are coveted by vacationers everywhere. Second, recreational activities abound by the sea. Activities such as surfing, diving, swimming, fishing, boating, boogie-boarding, and whale-watching all require water, while land-based activities such as hiking, biking, and camping, or airborne activities such as hang gliding and paragliding, can also be done at the seaside (with, some would say, enhanced views).

Those still in the workforce who are no longer shackled to their place of employment may seek to live by the seaside. Another category may also want to move there: the vast and burgeoning masses of retired people, including the bulge of baby boomers who are headed for retirement.

Therefore, it is my contention that in the coming years the value of seaside real estate is going to rise much faster than the comparable value of inland real estate.

And this trend has already started to happen worldwide. In the United States, the top 100 seaside counties have had population growth 50 percent higher than the national average from 1993 to 2000. I imagine the statistics are similar in other countries.

Bear in mind that with a higher than average population growth, property values will also rise faster than average. And remember, if property values nationwide have gone up by, say,

10 percent *on average*, and you are getting better than average, then you are doing all right!

So, if you agree that properties by the sea may rise in value faster than their inland counterparts, then I have a new question for you. . . .

What if you were to invest in real estate in those geographic areas where the growth in population was higher than average, in those demographic sectors that have higher than average growth, and furthermore where the properties were by the sea? Is it not possible that you would have an extremely high chance of beating the national average for property price increases?

Therefore, when I read that the value of properties went up on average by 7 percent, but company shares went up on average by a whopping 11 percent, I do not rush out to sell my properties and put the proceeds into the stock market. Frankly, I don't particularly care what the average increase of property values is (other than out of pure academic interest), as I know that my chances of greatly exceeding the average figures are, realistically, extremely high. I do not feel I would have any basis or evidence to assume I (or anyone else) can predict with the same level of confidence that they could similarly outperform the average returns on the stock market. Remember, in October of 1987, no one could tell me what was about to happen. And I am not even blaming my advisors: It is just a feature of the fast-moving (relative to property) stock market that such a big chunk of the market can be wiped out in a very short space of time.

Similarly, with the more recent decline of the Dow Jones index and particularly the decline of the strongly technology-weighted Nasdaq index, I don't recall anyone advising investors to get out. It would appear that the decline caught everyone by surprise. Beating the averages seems difficult.

So how do you beat the averages with property?

First, you are in an industry where the averages move slowly and predictably. The chances of the property market dropping in value across the board by 50 percent (the way they can with stocks) is very remote.

Second, by investing in those geographic locations where there has been sustainable growth greater than the national average, you position yourself well to also enjoy that higher than average growth.

Third, by investing in those sectors that outperform others, you can reasonably expect to further your greater than average returns.

None of this is rocket science. We could go into a country that neither of us has ever been to before, and within half an hour of talking with someone with a modicum of statistical knowledge, we would know which states, provinces, cities, and even suburbs to invest in to maximize our chances of beating that country's average returns. That to me seems like an incredibly huge advantage that is not only seldom exploited, but seldom mentioned, and certainly never by the detractors of property.

Keeping Your Eye on the Market

There is one further difference between investing in property and investing in other vehicles that I would like you to consider. . . .

Take people who trade currencies, futures contracts, options, and stocks.

Currencies fluctuate by the minute. A myriad of factors go into determining the value that the world places on each country's currency, and most of these factors change rapidly and often. Consequently, currency traders tend to spend their workday glued to their computer screens, Reuters monitors, and Bloomberg reports. Having your attention diverted could cost you a bundle! You really have to work this market minute by minute. Not surprisingly, most of the currency traders I have known were burnt out by the time they were thirty.

Futures contracts fluctuate less rapidly. Generally, if you keep your eye on the market several times a day, you will probably manage okay.

Further down the scale, options are traded all the time, but movements tend to not be as rapid as with futures contracts, and certainly not as rapid as with currencies. Monitoring things once a day is probably adequate for most investors.

Stocks generally tend to move slightly more slowly still. Unless you are staking your position based on small, daily movements, most stock market investors manage very well by monitoring their stocks once a week or even a couple of times a month.

Property, on the other hand, moves extremely slowly compared with all of the investments above. You could take a three-month cruise around Antarctica and not need to worry about your positions.

Imagine if the currency trader could not make it to work for a day, and there was no one to cover or work his positions. The losses could be devastating!

I have properties on other continents that I manage by remote control. If I spend three hours on any one of these properties per year, it's a lot! In other words, the management overhead is minimal. What's more, the three hours that I do put in are not scheduled regularly, but come up only if something happens to require my attention. The other markets, like currencies, futures, options, and stocks, may suffer if I do not monitor them actively for unexpected price movements.

So, wherever I am in the world, if someone says: "How would you like to take a week out of your schedule to go hiking in Patagonia?"—or to canoe down the Sepik River in Papua New Guinea, or to go hunting on the Forbidden Island, or to look at a deal, or to discuss a business proposal—I can do that without lying awake at night wondering if there has been another Black Monday (as in October 1987), or if the outbreak of a war somewhere has dramatically affected the value of my assets, or if my staff are making the decision that in their stead I would have made.

Property, when seen in this light, is relaxed, laid-back, solid, consistent, and sure. I did not say "slow but sure," for as we saw in Chapter 1, the growth potential of your invested capital in property can be spectacular. But you do not have to work it every nail-biting moment of the day.

Before finishing Part One, "Why Is Property So Good?," I want to address some of the niggling questions you may still have regarding investing in real estate. These are the questions that come up when you think: "Yes, that all sounds very interesting and convincing, but I have this burning question that I don't seem to be able to move beyond." I call these the "yes, but" questions.

Chapter 5

YES, BUT . . .

know from experience that even when I cover the ground that we have just covered in the chapters so far, there are many questions that keep popping up. One of the most common is:

"Yes, but where I come from, it is not possible to get 90 percent mortgages."

I would say: "Look around." You may be surprised which banks and institutions lend as much as 90 percent (even if it is not in their standard literature—after all, they would rather only give you a 50 percent mortgage, as their exposure would be lower).

Check out other banks and institutions. I am surprised at how many people only ever go to "their" bank (the one they have been with for twenty-three years) to ask for a mortgage, and when it is rejected, they complain to me that it doesn't work. Shop around!

Check out the Internet. There are many reputable lenders whose main portal is not through an office door but through the Web.

It may surprise you to know that you can get mortgages for more than 90 percent. In the Netherlands in the mid-1970s, mortgages of up to 125 percent were being offered. Banks and institutions were awash with money, and the theory was that when you bought a house, you would naturally want to renovate it to suit your own requirements. Such a renovation would increase the value of the property, so the banks would maintain collateral over the loan. Furthermore, they would have lent more of their surplus funds (which is what they wanted to do), and you would have a house entirely to your liking.

Often, when the loan-value ratio exceeds a certain breakpoint, banks will require you to take out mortgage guarantee insurance (sometimes known as private mortgage insurance or PMI), but this is a worthwhile expense if it gets you a high percentage mortgage.

"Yes, but that still doesn't work where I am from. Is there nothing else I can do?"

Of course there is. Your aim is not to secure as much of the loan as possible against the property being bought, but to borrow as much of the purchase price as possible. In other words, you don't care whether the loan is secured against the property you are buying, or against anything else.

So, let's assume that you can only get a mortgage for 70 percent of the purchase price. What would stop you from borrowing the remaining 30 percent against your own home (assuming you had such a home, and that you had equity in it, of course)? Nothing! What would stop you from asking a relative to let you use their equity to help secure your loan?

"Yes, but I don't own a home, and wouldn't dream of asking my relatives for some help. They would be insufferable in never letting me forget it!"

How about asking the seller to leave in 30 percent of the purchase price at 6 percent interest per annum for five years? There is no law against that. If the bank agrees to an 80 percent mortgage, then you could even pocket 10 percent in cash, to use as the deposit on your next investment.

"Yes, but then I would have borrowed 100 percent of the purchase price. Is there no law against that?"

No.

"Yes, but what if I lose my tenant? I have 100 percent borrowed, on which I am paying interest, and no money coming in. I will go bankrupt in no time at all!"

Get a new tenant. As we will see later in this book, if you have not had a tenant for more than a couple of weeks, it is not because the property is too small or too big or facing the wrong way or it has the wrong color carpet. You will only need to do one thing to attract a new tenant.

"Yes, but you said in Chapter 3 that if I depreciate an asset and then sell it for more than the written-down book value, that I have to pay depreciation recapture tax. What's the point in depreciating something if you have to pay it back later anyway?"

First off, you only ever pay depreciation recapture tax if you are silly enough to sell. If you never sell, it never comes into question

(just as with capital gains tax). Second, if you bought a property for $100,000, depreciated it down to $60,000, and then sold it for $200,000, it is not a foregone conclusion that you have to pay depreciation recapture tax on the $40,000 of claimed depreciation. The reason is that you never depreciated the land. It could well be that the value of the house itself has indeed declined, but that the land has gone up in value tremendously. In fact, you could sell for $200,000 and still claim a further depreciation on the dwelling if the facts back you up. Too often we settle for the gloomy answer.

But let's assume that you bought the property for $100,000 five years ago, depreciated it down to $60,000, and you can now sell it for $200,000. Are you worried that you will have to pay depreciation recapture tax on the $40,000 depreciation? At worst, you will have had an interest-free loan from the government that you have to repay only if you sell the property (if you never sell, you never pay back this loan). Where else can you get an interest-free loan? What's more, the dollars they "lend" you are hard (present-day) dollars, whereas the dollars you pay back are soft (future) dollars.

"Yes, but if I have to put up 30 percent of the purchase price in cash instead of only 10 percent, then my returns will not be magnified by a factor of 10 as you showed me in Chapter 1, but only by a factor of 3.33. Aren't you shortchanging me?"

This question shows me that we are making progress! At the beginning of this book, most readers find it difficult to believe that property can be much better than other investments. And now you are feeling shortchanged if you don't get more than 3.33 times the quoted returns!

I emphasize this inclination to say "*Yes, but . . .*" because that is how many people typically think. Every time I write a

new article or column on some aspect of real estate, or share a recent experience with property, I get a flurry of letters and e-mail from the "Yes, but" brigade, who seem to relish pointing out circumstances where what I say may not apply. It is as if they go out of their way to find a reason why it will not work. I guess for them, more often than not it doesn't.

Instead of proudly proclaiming with confidence:

"That won't work!"

or even saying:

"That won't work for me."

how about saying:

"How could I make that work for me?"

So destructive is the "Yes, but . . . way of thinking that Tony Robbins, in trying to get people to break this habit, gets the perpetrators, every time he catches them uttering it, to grab their own butts—literally. You soon learn to stop saying: "Yes, but . . ."!

Having fears when considering investing in real estate is natural. But letting that fear drive you is not productive. Developing the financial intelligence to be able to discern a good deal from a mediocre one, on the other hand, is wise.

With sufficient financial intelligence, you gain the confidence to do really well. And with that confidence comes daring. And when you dare to try, you practice. And through practice, you develop ability. And the more you exercise this newfound ability, the more your financial intelligence will go up as you learn new techniques, or nuances of old techniques. It becomes a positively reinforcing circle. You get better and better at it. At believing real estate is good, at finding great deals, at negotiating them, financing them, acquiring them, managing them, and watching them grow.

One day you may even wake up, realize that you are making more from property than from your regular job, and quit your job to work full-time on investing in real estate.

Chapter 6

SUMMARY: WHY INVEST IN REAL ESTATE?

n Part One of this book, I have presented why I believe property is so much better than other investments. I would summarize as follows:

You do not need much of the purchase price in cash to buy a property.

You can buy many dollars' worth of property more than you are paying for.

You can massively increase the value of a property without spending much money.

You do not need to sell a property to reap the benefits of any growth.

You do not need to monitor your properties from moment to moment like a hawk.

Property prices tend to increase relatively smoothly and consistently.

Property is very forgiving of mistakes.

Property has exceptional tax advantages.

The fluctuations of any one property relative to the national average are very low.

It is incredibly simple to do better than the national average for property.

It is the simplest, most reliable, and most consistent vehicle I know to convert even a little financial intelligence into a lot of cold, hard cash.

PART TWO

Okay! Show Me How to Do It!

Chapter 7

THE 100:10:3:1 RULE

Now that we have covered some of the reasons for getting into real estate, let's get to work and talk about the how-to.

Many people have considered investing in real estate. For some people, what this means is that they have looked at a couple of properties, or maybe even half a dozen, tried to figure out a way to make the deal work, and then given up, concluding that it was all too difficult.

So let me start by making one point very clear: Investing in properties is a numbers game, where the numbers involved are big. And I am not just talking about your profits! I am talking about the numbers of properties you must look at.

It can best be summed up in my global rule, which forms the title of this chapter:

The 100:10:3:1 Rule

What this rule says is that if you look at 100 properties, put offers in on 10, and try to arrange financing for 3, you *may* end up buying 1.

These are not just numbers pulled out of thin air. I have

found over the years, both through my own experiences and those of colleagues, associates, and students, that on average you must look at 100 properties in order to find ten worth putting offers in on. Good deals are not just there for the picking. You have to spend a bit of time sorting the wheat from the chaff. I will show you how to do that in the following chapters.

Of the ten offers that you submit, not all will be accepted. In fact, if you found that all your offers were being accepted, what would that tell you about your offers? Simply that you were offering way too much. You could have bought many of the properties for less than you were willing to pay.

So let's assume that of the ten offers you submitted to sellers, only three were accepted. Does this mean that you own three properties yet? Not quite, since you still have to arrange financing for them. (You would never pay cash! Why use up a lump of cash of, say, $100,000 to buy one $100,000 property, when you could buy four $100,000 properties using a $25,000 down payment and a $75,000 mortgage on each one?)

All right, so you try to arrange financing for these three properties. Again, it is no foregone conclusion that you will have all three properties successfully financed. Maybe only one will work. In this case, you will have looked at 100 properties to successfully buy one.

Of course, if none of the three works out, then how many more properties will you have to look at to buy another one? Another 100. Conversely, if all three are successfully financed, then no doubt you will be very happy.

This whole concept of looking at 100 properties in order to be able to buy one is a daunting concept for many people. You need perseverance to make this work. Let me explain what typically happens, especially to beginner investors.

Faced with the seemingly arduous task of looking at 100 properties, you get yourself all psyched up, and on your first Saturday, you go through listings from newspapers and real estate magazines, and go out and look at thirteen properties. So far so good!

The next weekend you excel yourself, and look at a whopping sixteen. You are doing well. You are nearly one third of the way there.

But the following weekend it's raining, and you are still a bit tired from the party the night before, so you defer looking to the weekend after. Except that weekend cousin Shirley is getting married, and you cannot no-show. The following weekend is the season finale of football, and you do not want to let your friends down by not going with them. The next weekend you promised to take your kids hiking, and you really enjoy that as well, so of course that takes priority! And then the weekend after that you announce (to yourself more than to anyone else) that this whole thing about looking at 100 properties does not work.

Your theory that this is impossible is validated!

It also works the other way around. We had a very humorous situation recently with one of my mentoring students. For a number of years I ran an educational program, where I took on a maximum of ten students from around the world for a twelve-month course on real estate that involved one-on-one mentoring complete with exercises and assignments.

At the first session, I told everyone about the 100:10:3:1 Rule, and that I expected everyone to go out and look at 100 properties during the course of the program. Margaret, one of the mentoring students, misunderstood me, and thought I meant that she had to look at 100 properties before the next one-on-one session in one month's time.

Guess which of the ten students was the first to look at properties? Guess which one was the first to put in an offer, and the first to successfully arrange financing on a property? Guess who was the first to buy one?

The fact that Margaret was the first to buy a great investment property is not important. As I told all the mentoring students, it was not a race. In fact, when Margaret learned that she had been working like crazy to meet the "very demanding" command by me to look at 100 properties in the first month, only to find out that she really had all year to do it, the anguish on her face was palpable. But instead of resting on her laurels and taking it easy for the rest of the year while her fellow students caught up, Margaret took the attitude that if she could do it in the first month, why not in subsequent months? She kept up her frenetic pace, not always reaching the 100 mark for each month (she also had a young family and a menagerie of animals to look after), but looking at a lot of properties nonetheless.

It should come as no surprise to you that by the end of that year's mentoring program, Margaret was a top performer.

Remember, buying properties is a numbers game. Look at a lot, and you will find some gems. Look at just a few, and you will find evidence to support the theory that "all the good ones have been taken."

It astounds me that people will spend more time, read more reports, compare more options, drive more miles, and talk with more sellers when looking for a new car that will cost money and depreciate during the few brief years of ownership than they will spend looking for an investment property that will appreciate and feed them forever.

The reason why it is so important to look at a whole lot of properties is that, in the process of looking at what's out there, you will get a gut feeling for what is the norm. You will know whether in the area you are looking it is normal to have two bathrooms, a double garage with an automatic garage door opener, and a quarter acre of land, or not. Then, when you stumble across a property with three bedrooms and a triple garage on half an acre of land that is selling for less than the others, you will know that in all probability this really is a bargain. You will know, from having looked at dozens and dozens of other properties, that you have found one that is worth investigating further.

If you did not look at 100 properties, how would you know what is good and what is not? How can you expect me to tell you what is a good buy in your area, when I may not even have been there in my life? How could I define a "good deal" for you? Imagine if I said that a garage is a requisite, when you lived in New York City where owning a car is not the norm? Or what if I said that air-conditioning was a real bonus, and you lived in Alaska or Iceland or Siberia? Clearly, what is desirable is entirely a relative concept. By looking at 100 properties in your target market, you will get a great understanding of what is a great deal and what is not.

Just what constitutes "looking at a property"? Does that mean looking at the text of an advertisement in the newspaper, or do you have to go to the property and spend an hour inspecting all the cupboards before you can say you have looked at it?

What I mean by "looking at a property" is evaluating it to the extent that you can explain either why you want to buy this property, or why you want to pass on it.

Let's assume that the very first property you stumble across after putting this book down is a $1 million property. One of the first things you may want to determine is whether or not the property, realistically, is in your price range. If you determine that you can only go up to $400,000 in purchase price, then you have "looked at this property," since according to my definition above, you can explain why you will pass on this property. However, don't kid yourself that you can now look at another 99 properties priced over $400,000 to meet my quota of 100!

Since you now know that you must look at properties below $400,000, then only those properties priced below that figure (or those properties where you think you can negotiate the price to below $400,000) qualify as part of your quota.

Similarly, if you have a reason not to buy on the west side of town, or near the expressway, or where there are fewer than three bedrooms, or any property without a pool, then you can only "look at" properties that meet your increasingly stringent criteria.

In this manner, you quickly narrow down the search to those properties that really are potential additions to your property portfolio. Each time you look at a property, you discover a reason why you should not buy it (for instance, the returns are not good enough), or, in the absence of any such reason, you have by default found a property that is a great buy.

By the time you have looked at ten properties, you are starting to get pretty specific as to what it is you are looking for. By the time you have looked at twenty, you will start to get a feel for what constitutes a good investment property. By the time you have looked at fifty, you may be getting excited about the few that were almost good enough for you.

Done in this way, once you have looked at 100 properties, you will be surprised at what you find.

Okay, so you are fired up! You believe in the advantages of property, and you accept that you have to look at 100 properties to buy one. And yet you may not have a clue where to start.

In the next chapter, we will cover how to find properties to look at. In the chapters following, we will look at how to evaluate them, how to negotiate them, how to put in offers, how to finance them, how to increase their value (massively) without spending much money, and finally how to manage them.

Chapter 8

FINDING PROPERTIES

There is no one magical source for great deals. I try to cover the field, and manage to find great investments using all kinds of mechanisms.

Classified Advertisements

The most easily overlooked source is simply the small column classified advertisements in the local newspaper. These are not the big display ads put in by the large real estate companies, but rather three- or four-line, single-column ads. The main reason why these may be a great way to find properties is that often this is the advertising method of choice used by owner-sellers who are not using a real estate agent.

Why do I like it when no real estate firm is involved? Because the chances are that the owner used his or her own resources to try to figure out the value of their property. Often they will be way above the market value, but by the same token, they will often be way below. That is an opportunity for you, assuming you know how to evaluate these properties.

Also, if an owner-seller has a sign up on their property, and they run a few ads themselves, then you will have less competition than if the property was listed with a real estate firm, as the firm would not only put a sign up on the property and run (much larger) ads in the newspapers, but they would also have the property, complete with photo, listed in their real estate magazine, in the computer system for their franchise organization, on the Web, and maybe even with a multiple listing service so that just about any agent or buyer can find it.

Finally, when you contact such an owner-seller, he will not have had nearly as many inquiries as an agent would have (had an agent been involved). So your offer may be more welcome than it otherwise would have been.

Even if a small column ad has been put in by a real estate agent, however, it is still worth pursuing: A great deal is a great deal, no matter how you stumbled across it.

One fabulous investment I came across many years ago was in fact advertised by a real estate agent as a column ad in the classified section of the newspaper. It concerned a tiny property (eighty-five square meters) on the corner of a busy intersection. It was the only commercially zoned property in a residential suburb, and had as the sole tenant a fish supply shop. The rental was $10,400 per annum, and the asking price was $59,000, giving a yield of 17.63 percent. By the time I spotted the advertisement, it was already late on a Sunday night. I phoned the number, and got the agent at home. I said to him, almost resigned: "I suppose this property has gone by now," fully expecting him to say, "Yes, and my phone hasn't stopped ringing all weekend." Instead, he replied that my call was in fact the first he had received on that property. We arranged to look at it at 8:00 the next morning.

There was nothing wrong with the property. It had high traffic flows past it, which was good for the tenant. The rent hadn't gone up for years, which was good for me (it meant that, in all probability, the rentals were below market levels).

In fact, the reason the owner was selling was that he was in poor health.

Normally, as you will see in the chapter on negotiations, I offer less than the asking price (what have you got to lose?). On this occasion, partially because it seemed such a good deal and I didn't want anyone else to beat me to it, and largely in deference to the health of the seller (who seemed to have factored that into the price in the first place), I agreed to pay the asking price.

I then went to the bank, told them I had bought a property that generated $10,400 in rent per annum, but that I didn't have a clue what it was worth. They went and looked at it, said it must be worth at least $80,000, and offered me a 70 percent mortgage.

Now, some of you will be thinking that 17.63 percent yield is good but not spectacular. My response is to remind you that I am not particularly interested in yields. With a mortgage of $56,000 (70 percent of $80,000) and a purchase price of $59,000, the total capital I had invested in this deal was only $3,000. The mortgage interest rate at the time of just under 10 percent meant I was paying $5,400 a year in interest. Because this was a commercial property, the tenant paid the outgoings (property taxes, insurance, etc.). Therefore, my net return was the rental income less the mortgage interest, or $5,000 per year. Given I only had $3,000 invested, my cash-on-cash return was in fact 167 percent per annum. In other words, I was pulling more out of this property every year than I had put into it in the first place.

What is more, the cash-on-cash return does not give a complete picture of how this property is performing, as it does not take into account extra expenses (such as maintenance) and other benefits (such as depreciation), or, for that matter, the capital growth. The internal rate of return (discussed later) for this property was even more impressive than the cash-on-cash return.

Now, it wasn't always a bed of roses. One winter there was a particularly heavy snowfall, and the veranda was so laden with snow that the whole thing came crashing down to the sidewalk. Luckily no one was around at the time. It cost $2,500 to replace. In cash terms, that wiped out half of my profit for the year from that property (and reduced my cash-on-cash return to a paltry 83.33 percent). However, in actual fact, because most of the $2,500 cost of replacing the veranda was a repair (and therefore deductible against income) and the rest was considered an improvement over the original veranda (and therefore could be added to the capital value of the property and depreciated), the after-tax situation was not that bad, and my returns still exceeded 100 percent for the year.

To this day I still own the property. It has never had a week of vacancy, and is slowly increasing in value with time. I am the first to admit that the profits from this property would not pay for the services of a butler or the parking of a Learjet at the airport, but the whole point is that small, classified advertisements often have wonderful opportunities.

Real Estate Magazines

Real estate magazines are a preferred source of listings, as these days they nearly all have color photos included with each listing, and therefore the advertiser cannot skillfully use words to hoodwink you into believing that a dump is a fabulous mansion. You can very quickly look through many properties, and based on your knowledge of the area the property is in, the stated number of rooms, the asking price, and the general look of it in the photo, you can make a decision as to whether it is worth looking at in more detail.

"Looking at it in more detail" may simply mean phoning the real estate firm involved. A couple of questions can soon let you know whether to abandon this property and move on to another one, or whether to continue the research into this property. Valid questions could be "Why are the sellers quitting?" "What are the rental levels in that area?" "How have property values shifted in this area in recent times?" and "What is the population growth here?"

Once, between Christmas and New Year, I was looking through a real estate magazine in New Zealand (the kind that are given away free from stands outside real estate firms and in shopping malls). Being in the Southern Hemisphere and therefore the summer holiday season, it was an extra-thick issue with hundreds of listings. Each listing had a color photograph, a brief description, and contact details of the agent concerned. And there I found at the bottom of a page, surrounded by homes with asking prices of $200,000 to $400,000, a small two-bedroom cottage, literally a two-minute walk from the center of Queenstown (a popular and beautiful summer and winter resort playground), with the curious wording: "Offers over $20,000 considered."

I contacted the agent, half expecting her to say that there was a typo in the asking price. But to my surprise, she reported that the owner had fled the country owing lots of people money, and that the bank just wanted to get rid of it.

In talking with her, I said that I found it curious that she was asking for offers over $20,000. I asked her: "When you ask for offers over X, does anyone ever offer you X plus $5,000 or X plus $10,000?"

She admitted that no one ever offered more than the suggested minimum. Not surprisingly, I limited my offer to $20,000.

Two weeks went by, and I hadn't heard anything. I had almost given up on it, when I got a letter from the bank that held the mortgage. They complained to me that I should well know that the property was worth a lot more than $20,000, and suggested I come back with a sensible offer.

I replied that it was only their contention that the property was worth a lot more than $20,000. A property, so I continued, is not necessarily worth what a seller thinks it is worth (they may have unrealistic expectations), or for that matter what a buyer thinks it's worth (a buyer wants it for a song). A property is not always worth what a real estate agent suggests—some may suggest a high price to get the listing, or a low price to effect a quick sale. A property is not necessarily worth what an appraiser thinks it is worth—some may suggest a price on the high side to appease a seller, or a price on the low side to appease a buyer. And a property is certainly not always worth what a bank thinks it's worth. Rather, a property is only worth that price at which a willing buyer and a willing seller agree to transact the property. And if the bank really thought that it was worth a lot more than $20,000, so I suggested, they should go out and find a buyer who agreed with them. In the meantime, to show that I was still an earnest buyer, I raised my offer to $22,000.

Do you think they suddenly accepted my offer?

No, they didn't. They wrote back, and said that if I was willing to raise my offer to $22,500, we had a deal.

By going up another $500, they most likely felt they could save face to some extent. They could always say that I tried to get it for a ridiculous price, but that they made me come up to their level. I have no problem with that, so I agreed to $22,500. But I had bought a property sight unseen.

I had a tradesman who did work for me in Queenstown, and asked him to check out the property. He said it was generally in good shape, but that it needed a new front door and a new shower stall. Twenty minutes later he called again and asked: "Are you aware that there is a new front door and a new fiberglass shower in the cellar?" I replied that I didn't even know it had a cellar!

The cottage was painted and generally spruced up and was immediately rented for $130 per week, or $563 per month. The yield was therefore 30.03 percent.

Many months later I was down in Queenstown on business, and went to inspect my $22,500 property (to this day the cheapest I have ever bought). The property manager I use took me through it. I commented on the nice furniture and kitchen appliances. "Yes," he said, "you've done well!"

I replied: "You mean the tenants."

"Oh no," he said. "All that is yours." Unbeknownst to me, as part of the original purchase, I had acquired a kitchen table with four chairs, a microwave oven, a stove, cutlery, crockery, beds, mattresses, freestanding wardrobes, a couch, and numerous other household items.

The property was not perfect in every way. For instance, the land was not freehold, but leasehold. That means that I pay an annual lease fee (of around $1,500). However, since I do not own the land, and since land is the only thing that you cannot depreciate for tax purposes, I could depreciate the entire purchase price of $22,500.

Soon after I got back home, I bumped into a friend who asked me what I had been up to. Full of enthusiasm, I related the story of the cottage. My friend hit her fist into the palm of her other hand and exclaimed: "Darn! I saw that ad but thought it was a typo!"

Remember, just because something seems too good to be true doesn't necessarily mean that it is.

I still have many unanswered questions related to this property. Why did the owner not try to sell it for more? Why was the property not listed at a higher price (in which case more people might have thought it was viable and would have responded)? Why did the real estate agent involved not buy the property, or tip off a friend or acquaintance that there was a deal going down cheaply?

Who knows, and in a sense, who cares? The fact is that these sorts of deals happen all the time. Just because a bargain property has been listed in a real estate magazine that is displayed and distributed from countless real estate agents' premises, and read by thousands of agents and buyers, does not mean that you will not be able to acquire it. You can find properties that offer spectacular returns no matter how well advertised they are.

By the way, just as with the $59,000 commercial property, I still own the Queenstown cottage to this day. It is still chugging along, generating between $100 and $150 per week (depending on the season) of passive income. The internal rate of return is phenomenal. I still claim depreciation every year (the written-down book value is getting pretty low!). And, just as with the $59,000 commercial property, on its own it may not pay for much, but I am sure you will agree that if you have enough of these small, great performers that you never sell, then combined they amount to something worth having.

Real Estate Agents

If classified advertisements and real estate magazines give you a huge pool of properties to consider and the occasional phenomenal bargain from publicly available sources, then real estate agents offer you an ongoing stream of good recommendations that are not always out in the open yet. A real estate agent worth his salt will know what you are looking for, and not waste your time with properties that you would turn down in a hurry.

That brings us to the question of how you should go about choosing a real estate agent.

One: Never stick to just one agent. Why would you? One lone agent does not have access to every property on the market, and he or she does not get to hear on the grapevine about every deal that is coming up.

Two: Work with agents who are themselves investors. I know that sounds counterproductive, on the basis that if the agent were to stumble across a bargain, he or she is hardly likely to offer it to you. On the face of it that is true, but there is a limit to how many properties agents will buy (they have this constant dilemma between selling properties to earn a commission and buying them for the long haul). Most important, real estate agents who are themselves investors know what it is that you are after in a property. They will not waste your time telling you how gorgeous the view of the garden is from the living room, or how cozy it seems at night, or how the deli up the road has great liverwurst on Sunday mornings. They will provide you with the things you want to know—growth in population in that area, growth in rentals, vacancy rates, property taxes, and other such factors.

So how do you find a good real estate agent? The simple answer is to interview them. You may receive a recommendation from someone, but if not, you can always try some at random. Just as looking at properties is a numbers game, so is finding a good real estate agent that you are happy to work with. You might interview fifty to find four or five that you can work with regularly for a long time.

One exercise I get the mentoring students to do is go to a real estate office where they have never been before (any office picked at random in an area where they have determined they want to invest), and ask: "Who would be the best agent to deal with concerning investment properties?" If there is a lot of foot-shuffling and blank stares, go to another office. But if someone volunteers or is volunteered, ask him or her the simple question: "What is the best investment property that you have on your books at present?"

If he identifies one, then you are 10 percent on your way to finding a good agent. I say only 10 percent, because you still have to ask the following qualifying question: "Why?" In other words, why does he think that the property he has just pointed out is the best investment property on his books.

If he says: "Because the decor is so tastefully done" or "The neighborhoods are so lovely," then you have to move on. But if he says: "Well, this property sold five years ago for $328,000 or about the same as similar properties at the time. Today it is on the market at $415,000, but other comparable properties have been selling for over $500,000. What is more, the owners have received approval to pop the top and add another story, and rentals in the area have been strong. Vacancy rates are uniformly low." Then, whether or not the property is a good deal for you, you know you are dealing with an agent who can speak your investor language. This will make life a lot easier for you.

Those real estate agents who do not speak your language can make life very frustrating for you, and can seem to inhibit your ability to invest. Take heart! They also make it frustrating for your competition!

This was brought home to me in the early 1990s. I had spotted a newspaper advertisement for a block of three shops in a popular seaside community. The quoted yield seemed high, so I asked the agent to confirm that a local tax had not inadvertently been included in the quoted rentals. She replied (erroneously) that the tax did not apply to commercial property, and suggested I visit the butcher in the end shop, as he was the owner and seller.

I duly visited him in his shop. There were no customers. To start off with, I asked him why he was selling the building, and he replied that he was far too busy to talk and referred me back to his real estate agent. So much for making it easy for me to buy, especially when you consider that his business was in trouble (it went into liquidation soon after I bought the building).

I went back to the agent, and said that I had done my own research, and that I was ready to put in an offer. Could I submit it that afternoon?

This was the middle of December, and her answer stunned me. "No," she said, "I cannot do that, as I am packing to go away on vacation."

"Wow!" I said, "must be some vacation. Where are you going? To Europe for six months?" She replied that she was only going down the road for a few days, but was adamant that she was too busy.

"Great!" I thought. She is going away, and will not come back until just before Christmas when everything is shutting down. Furthermore, the owner is hardly likely to sell the building without her, given his attitude during my brief visit to his shop. Therefore, their perception of the pool of buyers will be artificially low, and their expectation of price will be diminished accordingly.

She did not submit my offer until January 11, by which time I had dropped it another couple of tens of thousands. It was the only offer they had received. I fully expected them to counter, but it was accepted as is.

Sometimes, when the other side seems slow, not focused, or not motivated, it can really work in your favor.

"Well, what about the butcher who went under just after you bought the building?" I can hear you ask. Good question. Before I heard that he had closed his doors for the last time, I got an inquiry from a woman to say that the shop seemed empty, and that it would make a great delicatessen. Could she take on a lease? At first I thought she must have been talking about another building, but it soon became apparent that she wasn't: The butcher shop was indeed empty. She signed up for a 12-year lease, and spent more than $30,000 renovating the premises. It is still a delicatessen/coffee shop to this day, and yes, as with the other properties discussed earlier, I still own it. Why wouldn't I? It still generates passive income, its income and capital value continue to go up, I have refinanced it to pull out some money, and by not selling, I have no depreciation recapture tax issues or capital gains tax issues to worry about.

Another example of how a "slow" real estate agent can work in your favor concerns a funeral parlor I came across in a country town. While I had been out of the country, this particular property got passed in at an auction at $195,000. It was a custom-built funeral parlor, which meant it had a waiting room, a chapel, a slumber room, a viewing room, a mortuary, and a chilling room (no marks for guessing what they kept cool in there). However, the operators had left the industry, and the building was empty. What else can you do with a funeral parlor? There are not many alternative uses that I could think of. A theme restaurant (vegetarian, of course) would seem very distasteful.

So I had someone call every funeral operator in the country, to ask them if they wanted to expand into this town. Most said no, some laughed out loud, and one said: "Yes! I've always wanted to operate in that town."

I signed the funeral operator up on an agreement such that if I should become the owner of the building, he would then become the tenant. Already, the building was worth more to me (with a committed tenant) than it was to the seller (who had only an empty building).

Anyway, I went to see the real estate agent involved. It was a cold winter afternoon when I drove into town, and when I got to his office, his receptionist told me that he was busy, and would be for at least another half-hour. I told her I would be back, and spent the next half-hour walking in the rain. When I got back, I was told that he was still on the phone, and was likely to be so for some time more. I replied that that was fine, and that I would simply wait in the reception area.

Eventually he came out, and asked me gruffly what it was I wanted. I replied that I wanted to look at the funeral parlor premises. We arranged to meet there in yet another hour. More time in the rain.

Sometime during this tour, I think the agent realized that I was serious after all about the building. He asked me if I wanted to go through it again, perhaps with him, or perhaps on my own. I replied that I had seen it, and that we should get back to his office to write up a contract.

"You can't do that!" he exclaimed.

"Why not?" I asked.

"Because the seller wants to lease a small portion of another building on the property, and you would have to figure out a rental value for that portion."

I told him that I already had a figure in mind, and that we would just include it in the wording of the offer. I asked him to start writing up the offer. He hesitated, and seemed unable to fathom my speed or direction. So I offered to write it up myself. He agreed, and his relief was obvious.

It seemed to me that the agent was just not ready for a sale. Who on earth would want an empty funeral parlor?

Of course, for me it wasn't empty. I acquired the entire property for a net figure of $170,000. I told the bank that that's what I had paid for it, but that I now had two tenants. One, the funeral parlor operator, was signed up on a 10 + 10 year lease (ten years with a right of renewal for another ten years), and the other, the seller, was signed up on a 6 + 6 year lease, for a total rental of $30,500 per annum. Therefore, so I told the bank, it might be worth more than what I paid. The bank sent in their own appraiser, valued it at $240,000, and gave me a 66 percent mortgage of $160,000. So in this case, I had only $10,000 of my own capital tied up in the property, while I was receiving $30,500 in rent, less $15,500 in mortgage interest, for a net $15,000. While the net yield on the purchase price was a "modest" 17.94 percent ($30,500/$170,000), my cash-on-cash return was in fact 150 percent ($15,000/$10,000). Once again I was pulling more out of this property every year than I had put in as a one-off at the beginning.

Apart from showing that even an empty funeral parlor can offer some attractive passive income streams, the point here is that the attitude of the real estate agent did not help to make a sale, which of course worked in my favor. It's a bit like when there is a lot of red tape to deal with: It makes it difficult to do business, but it also makes it difficult on your competition. So long as you have some degree of perseverance, you can easily leave competitors way behind.

When the people I deal with are fast, knowledgeable, and efficient, I am grateful for the ease with which the work at hand can get done. And when the people I deal with are, to put it politely, in the wrong profession, then I am grateful that most of my potential competition packs up and goes away. You win either way. This is a much healthier way of looking at it than saying that astute agents will never sell you a bargain (as they would buy it themselves) and that slow people will never offer you a bargain (as they couldn't find one if they wanted). Once again, whatever you believe is what will manifest itself for you.

To finish off our discussion on real estate agents, bear in mind that just as you want to deal with an astute agent, a good agent will like to have an astute investor to work with. People who buy homes to live in tend to buy on average only once every five years (and most of them own only one home to live in at a time). But an investor may buy one a month, or three in a good week. That is more interesting (financially!) for a real estate agent. Once you have found a cluster of astute, like-minded real estate agents, you will find that you tend to stick with each other for a long time.

Off-Market Sales

So far in considering how to find properties, we have only considered those advertised in newspapers or real estate magazines, and those listed through real estate agents. There is another category altogether, namely properties where the owners do not even know they want to sell.

The presence of a "For Sale" sign on a property is a clear indication that the owners want to sell. However, the absence of such a sign does not necessarily indicate that they do not want to sell. There is only one way to find out: Knock on the door and ask.

I am not suggesting you go up and down every street asking all the property owners if they want to sell. You would waste a lot of time and make a general nuisance of yourself. However, if you have identified a property as being particularly well suited to your needs (meaning the needs of a potential or prospective tenant), then there is no law against you asking the current owner if he would consider selling. In particular, if the value of the property to you is a lot more than the value to the present owner, then it could well be a win-win situation.

For example, you may own a property that has a large backyard, but you cannot drive a car down between the house and the boundary fence. By buying the property next door, and creating a right-of-way or easement, you may gain car access to the rear of both properties.

Similarly, right now I am looking at a commercial building in downtown Phoenix. It is a beautiful art deco building with a historic places designation on it (meaning tax breaks for anyone renovating it). One concept is to turn it into condominium apartments, but the downside is that there would not be sufficient parking. So I am looking at the building next door. It is an old building, in a terrible state of repair, and is used as a transients' hotel. It will probably not be there much longer. As a hotel, it has limited value. However, as the site for a potential parking garage for the condominiums next door, it has great value. Therefore, the potential value to me may be much more than the value to the current owners. There is no "For Sale" sign on it, but I would be foolish to limit my search to those buildings that are officially on the market.

Does this mean that every property owner I approach with an offer welcomes the offer with open arms? Of course not! I am rejected more often than not. But the few times you are welcomed makes all the rejections worthwhile.

Write Your Own Advertisements

Often in life, we sit waiting for good things to come our way. However, generally speaking, no one will ever come up to you and say: "If you sign this contract to buy this property, you will instantly increase your net worth by $100,000, have an annual income (indexed for inflation) of $12,000, and you do not even need to put any money into the deal." The deals themselves exist, but you have to go out and find them.

Therefore, if you agree that you need to expend some effort in finding your deals, why wait until someone else has become motivated enough to place an advertisement in the paper, or to approach a real estate agent? Why not take the initiative, and run your own advertisements offering to *buy* properties?

Your advertisement may read something like:

> **Serious investor wants to buy properties.**
> **Maintenance or repairs no problem.**
> **Quick decisions. Phone (123) 555-1234.**

You may run this advertisement in your local paper and get no response, or you might get dozens of responses. Change the wording to see what works in your area. Often, people want quick results. When they read your advertisement, they may think: "Wow, if I call this person, it could just save me the bother, hassle, and expense of going through a real estate agent, signing all kinds of documents, and possibly being taken for a ride. What have I got to lose?"

You may even consider other ways of advertising your willingness to buy properties. Once I spoke at a seminar at a large hotel in Los Angeles. As I drove up to the lobby, I saw a large van in the parking lot with the words "WE BUY HOUSES" boldly painted on the side of the van in fluorescent green, along with the phone number. Not surprisingly, the owner of this business was in the audience. I asked him whether the advertising worked, and he replied that he was bemused but happy that no one else was doing it. When he handed me his business card, the most prominent thing on it was not his name or title, but rather the words "WE BUY HOUSES" again. Very memorable.

Let the world know that you are in the market to buy investment properties!

Other Sources of Property Listings

There are many other sources of property listings that, with time, may work better for you than all the methods described above. Once people get to know that you are a serious property investor, then they will catch some of your fever. For instance, your cousin hears that his neighbor has got his property on the market, and the price does seem rather cheap to your cousin, so he calls you up and suggests you take a look at it. Or a friend phones you to say that he just bought a beachfront property, and that there are a couple of other properties on the market that seem underpriced. He would like you as a holiday-home neighbor anyway, so he calls you about it. People come out of the woodwork to offer you deals, merely because they know you invest in property.

Hilariously, after I bought the funeral parlor, I received at least one phone call a week for months from people wanting to know if I wanted to buy their (or their client's) funeral parlor as well. They all thought that I "invested in funeral parlors," rather than great property deals. None of the other parlors had anything to offer that interested me, so I only ever bought that one. And yes, I still own it.

Many years ago, I was asked in New Zealand to talk to a group of real estate agents from Harcourts, the country's largest real estate company, about what an investor is looking for in a property. At the time I never thought that there would be anything in it for me, but I went along anyway. Unbeknown to me, the national training coordinator for Harcourts was in the audience. She said at the end that what I had said was very interesting, and asked me if I would like to teach all their agents throughout the country. I remember telling her: "I want to buy property, not teach you people how to sell it." But she reasoned with me that if I were to teach their agents around the country, I would get to see an awful lot of great properties, and meet with many of the top agents. And of course she was right. In this way, teaching what an investor is after was a great vehicle for me to look at more than my quota of properties. The numbers game was working.

That is not to say that you have to teach agents in order to find properties to buy. But it does reinforce the concept that property is a numbers game. The more properties you get to look at or consider, through whatever mechanisms are available, the greater the likelihood that you will find your next deal that sounds too good to be true.

Chapter 9

ANALYZING DEALS

S o, let's have a reality check. You believe (for now, anyway!) that property is worth pursuing further. You agree that you have to commit to the 100:10:3:1 Rule to succeed. You have worked the various methods of finding properties. And now you have a short list of properties that you think *may* be good, but for the life of you, you cannot determine which really are great, and which only appear good. You do not know whether to be cautious about buying one, or whether you should be clamoring to buy them all.

It's time we learned how to analyze properties.

Yield

As we saw in Chapter 2, the yield is simply the rental income divided by the purchase price. It is not very interesting for the simple reason that it takes no account of how much cash we have put into the property.

Cash-on-Cash Return

Imagine a property costs $100,000, and that the rental income is $10,000 per annum. Then, by definition, the yield is 10 percent.

But the return on your money will be 10 percent only if you put up the entire purchase price in cash. If you only put up a deposit of $30,000, and got a mortgage for the remaining $70,000, then the return on your investment would now be $10,000 less the mortgage interest, divided by a capital outlay of only $30,000. If the mortgage interest is, say, 7 percent, then the mortgage payment would amount to $4,900. Your return would then be $5,100/$30,000, or 17 percent.

Notice that the property is the same, the purchase price is the same, the rental income is the same, and yet the "return" has gone from 10 percent to 17 percent. And we have only just started, because we still haven't taken account of property taxes, maintenance, property manager fees, the vacancy rate, repairs, gardening, principal repayments, mortgage application fees, appraisal fees, or spiderproofing, to name just a few expenses. Nor have we taken into account the depreciation you can claim, and the subsequent increase to your cash flow.

If we were to take all these factors into account, then we would have a pretty good picture—a snapshot in fact—of how this property will perform *at any one moment in time*. Certainly, the cash-on-cash return is far more useful than the yield in determining if a property is a good investment. Nonetheless, it is still just a *snapshot*. What we really want is a *motion picture* that enables us to *see into the future*.

Internal Rate of Return

Remember how we said that the yield was a simplistic measure of a property's performance, since it didn't take into account the fact that you may not pay cash for a property?

The cash-on-cash return does take account of the fact that you are borrowing part of the purchase price. But it also has its limitations.

What if you know that the rents on your property are going to increase by 50 percent next year? This crucial piece of knowledge is not reflected in the yield or the cash-on-cash return, as they both just consider the current rent. Similarly, neither the yield nor the cash-on-cash returns are changed, even if we know that the property will double in value over the next eighteen months.

If the cash-on-cash return looks at all the cash flows into and out of a property at any one point in time (the snapshot), the internal rate of return looks at how the cash flows and property value change with time (the motion picture). To do this, it takes into account what the projected growth in rentals will be, what the capital growth is expected to be, what the mortgage interest payments will be, given that the principal is slowly being paid off, and what depreciation can be claimed each year.

For instance, using our $100,000 investment property, it may be determined that the net after-tax cash flow out of the property is, for argument's sake, $1,000 per year for each of the next five years. At the end of this time, the property may be expected to be worth $150,000, based on the expected capital growth rates. Our equity (what we own in the property, or the market value less the mortgage) may then be, say, $85,000.

The cash flow sequence (the motion picture) would therefore be: $30,000 in at purchase (the down payment), $1,000 out for each of the next five years, and then an equity at the end of $85,000.

The internal rate of return is that return that a bank would have to give you, such that if you gave the bank $30,000, they could give you $1,000 for each of five years, and at the end of five years, give you $85,000.

Like it or not, in our hypothetical property, that is exactly the cash flow sequence that we are facing. $30,000 in, $1,000 out for each of five years, and then $85,000 out. What is more, the IRR takes the time value of money into account. A dollar today is worth more than a dollar in a year's time (that is why if I owe you money, you want it now, and not in a decade or two).

Thus, even though the yield is an accurate measure, it is not very illuminating. The cash-on-cash return gives us a far more detailed and clear picture of how a property is performing, but like the yield, it is still only a snapshot of one instant in time when you look at this property.

The IRR is by far the most interesting measure, as it takes the future into account.

Of course, while the yield is easy to work out on the back of an envelope, and while the cash-on-cash return is easy to work out on a calculator, the IRR would be almost impossible to work out on the back of an envelope, and extremely difficult on a calculator. Fortunately, computers are perfect for the job, and you can now determine the IRR of a prospective investment property in no time at all.

With appropriate software, you can, in about one minute flat, put in the pertinent financial details of a property, and then see the yield, the pretax cash flow into or out of the property, the after-tax cash flow, the buildup in equity, and the internal rate of return.

To do this, the software must take account of all the relevant factors that will influence your cash flows and buildup of equity. These will include:

- purchase price
- renovation costs
- true market value
- closing costs
- rental income
- vacancy rates
- expected capital growth rate
- expected inflation of rents and expenses

- mortgage interest rate
- mortgage structure (interest only or principal and interest)
- property management fees
- property taxes
- maintenance
- repairs
- mortgage application fees
- your income level
- prevailing tax rates

When all these factors are put into the software, then the results (both the numbers and the graphs) will give you an insight that would be almost impossible to get any other way. Some properties that seemed great when you inspected them are suddenly shown to be lemons. Conversely, properties that seemed marginal can turn out to be great performers.

Furthermore, if you want to know how your property would perform if the rent went down by 5 percent or $200 a month, you can easily do that. Similarly, you can see what would happen if the mortgage interest went up, or if your expenses ballooned. This is called doing a sensitivity analysis.

Once you have used the software, it is difficult to attempt to evaluate properties without it! It's a bit like driving at night without your headlights.

The other thing about the software is that the internal rate of return that it generates is dimensionless. This is a fancy way of saying that it is just a number. It is a percentage that you can compare with the internal rate of return on any other property. In other words, you can compare the IRR on a $140,000 property with a 90 percent mortgage at 7 percent interest to the IRR on a $650,000 property with a 40 percent mortgage at 5 percent interest, and get a fair comparison, even if they are in different countries where the tax rates and management fees are different.

Our popular software package REAP (Real Estate Acquisition Program) is available on our Web site at www.dolfderoos.com. It enables you to quickly evaluate a potential investment property, perform sensitivity analyses, and print reports that are useful for mortgage applications. A demo version of REAP is also available, complete with an audio-visual tutorial explaining every aspect of the program.

Other Factors to Consider

While I place a lot of importance on the internal rate of return, there are of course other factors that should always be considered when buying a property. As most real estate books will tell you, the top three criteria for a property are: Location, Location, Location! But just what constitutes a good location where you are looking may be somewhat of a subjective thing. For residential properties, generally it is desirable to be located near schools (but not backing onto them!), near the shops (but not beside them), and with good access to freeways or arterial routes. However, since it is so subjective, it is risky for me to dictate what you should look for in your area.

Remember, part of the trick is to find a property with a twist. If you can find property for a song that backs onto a schoolyard, don't reject it just because you recall me writing somewhere that you don't want to back onto a schoolyard. A bargain is a bargain, and your tenants may just have two kids who go to that school and consider the proximity a bonus.

Keep looking at many properties. Expect to look at 100 to find one to buy. The more you look at, the easier it is to develop a gut feeling for whether a particular property will be a good performer or not. If you decide to use the software, it will further speed up the process. You will begin to develop a nose for a good property.

Even if you are in unfamiliar territory, you will be able to make surprisingly astute investment decisions. In fact, often there is an advantage in being from out of town. The locals all are limited by their perceptions of what is a "good" area and what is not. You, on the other hand, are just concerned with the numbers. If the cash flow and the growth prospects are good, then you may be able to find a bargain because you have not been somewhere long enough to absorb the local snobbery. And I'll guarantee you one thing: Once a dollar is in your bank account, it does not matter (and no one will ask you) if it came from a posh part of town or an average one.

Chapter 10

NEGOTIATIONS AND SUBMITTING OFFERS

I f all aspects of property investment that we have covered up until now seem a bit like cranking a handle, then the negotiation phase of property investment is where you can really let your creativity and imagination run wild.

The rules and regulations that cover most other transactions are spelled out in great detail and adhered to under threat of fines and ostracism from the game. For example, when you go to an auction of merchandise, from a local secondhand dealer's to Sotheby's, the rules are read out, one by one, and people are often given a copy (just in case they couldn't hear properly) as a backup. The rules spell out how you must bid, what constitutes a valid bid, what happens the moment the hammer falls, how much you will pay as a deposit, in which form you will make the payment, when and how you will pay the balance, when and from where you must collect the articles bought, and what they will do to you if you get anything wrong. If you like living by other people's rules, auctions must be heaven!

Similarly, when you deal in stocks, options, futures, certificates of deposit, treasury bills, mutual funds, term loans, bank deposits, or annuities, the rules are numerous, rigid, and strictly enforced.

This contrasts sharply with real estate. As I alluded to in Part One of this book, property is unique in that you can include just about anything you want in the negotiations. And people often do!

Remember the funeral parlor I bought? The offer I wrote out in front of the reluctant agent had a clause whereby the seller agreed to lease a specific portion of the premises comprising 800 square feet at $6.25 per square foot plus outgoings (property taxes, insurance, etc.) for a period of six years with a right of renewal for a further six years, with rent reviews (upward only) occurring every two years.

The seller countered the offer by stipulating that the canvas awning over the front door would remain his property at the end of the lease. So here we are negotiating a $170,000 property, and part of the negotiations concern a canvas awning that will probably need to be replaced several times during the twelve-year lease period.

I felt like countering this offer by stipulating that the seller mow my lawn every Sunday for three months after the purchase, but thought better of it. The whole point is that you can put in a contract anything that you like, and people often do.

I have seen worn-out BMWs firing on only three cylinders included in property contracts. I have negotiated with sellers, incumbent tenants, and prospective tenants for cleaning contracts, repairs to premises, remodeling jobs, the removal of some buildings, and even loans.

A great lesson can be learned on how you can put anything in a real estate contract from one particular property I bought back in 1993. In a small classified advertisement, a real estate agent had simply advertised: "Commercial property, $12,000, 17% yield, phone XXX-XXXX."

Just like with the $59,000 fish shop, and the $22,500 cottage in Queenstown, this sounded too good to be true, but I phoned nonetheless. In case you are wondering whether I ever phone such an advertisement to find out that there is in fact a typo, the answer is a resounding yes. In fact, I would say that for every twenty calls I make where the deal sounds too good to be true, probably nineteen of them are. However, the twentieth deal usually makes the time wasted phoning the other nineteen hopefuls worthwhile. Those odds are pretty good, in fact—much better than the odds faced by people who buy lottery tickets, and yet the lotteries attract the masses, and what I do is considered bizarre by most people. Indeed, when I open a newspaper to look at real estate, I consider it a bit of a lottery, with the difference that I know that, in all probability, there are several winners right there on the page staring at me.

Anyway, in this particular case, the agent told me that there was indeed a typographical error, and that the purchase price was in fact $120,000, not $12,000 as advertised. However, since the rental was $20,000 per annum, the yield was still 17 percent.

The property in question was a restaurant, built in a beautiful log-cabin-style home. It was the only commercial premise in picturesque Cass Bay, about a twenty-minute drive outside Christchurch, New Zealand. The owner wanted to stay on as the tenant, and was willing to sign a five-year lease with three rights of renewal for periods of five years each.

We negotiated a deal at $120,000. A couple of months later, as the closing day (settlement) approached, the seller contacted me and said, rather undiplomatically: "You will have to pay me $130,000 instead of $120,000 for the property."

I just about fell off my chair! Here we had a contract, and the seller was sounding as though he wished to renege on the original deal. Now I am sure that many people will relish such a situation, and say: "Sue him!" But in my experience, litigation is not a good way to increase or improve in any way your passive income. Rather, it just tends to increase the active income of the attorneys involved.

I said to my seller: "Why?"

He replied that he simply could not pay off his mortgagee and satisfy other debts secured against the property unless he had a sale price of $130,000.

Now before you read on, ponder for a moment what you might have done in this situation. It seemed apparent that he didn't have any equity at all, so canceling the deal and suing for specific performance (his inability to meet his contractual obligations) would probably not have netted much.

I started by asking: "What's in it for me?"

He said that he would be willing to pay $22,000 in annual rent instead of $20,000. In other words, I would get a return of 20 percent on the extra $10,000 capital outlay he required for me to acquire the property. It seemed that the business could support such a rental. Would you have agreed to this?

I did not. I told him that I would not pay him $10,000 extra, but that I would *lend* him $10,000. The rental would still go up to $22,000 per annum, and he would have to repay the $10,000 loan on the earliest of (1) the expiry of his lease, (2) his default of the lease (if he doesn't pay the rent), or (3) his assignment of the lease (if he sells the business). Just for security, I put in the contract that I would hold a chattel mortgage over his restaurant equipment.

Five weeks later he sold the business, and I got my $10,000 back. The rental meanwhile stayed at $22,000.

You can write your own rules with real estate (so long as you can reach an agreement with the other party). In the case of the restaurant, despite a situation that on the surface seemed unable to be resolved, both the seller and I got what we wanted out of the deal. He got the extra money he needed to pay off his debt secured against the property (he paid me back out of the proceeds of the sale of his business). And I still paid only $120,000 for the property as originally agreed upon. Plus of course I was collecting $2,000 extra in rent. After the business was sold, my yield therefore went up to 18.33 percent ($22,000/$120,000). My cash-on-cash return, while not over 100 percent as in previous examples, was still a healthy 55 percent.

Your ability to write just about anything into a real estate contract is one of the most overlooked and underrated advantages of real estate investing.

As part of my negotiations with the seller of a property, I usually incorporate the following four concepts. They are not always mandatory or even appropriate, but I use them often.

1. Do not always write up the contract in your own name. There are many ownership structures you can use to acquire properties: in your own name, in companies, family trusts, partnerships, and as joint owners. Since I may not know what the best entity will be for a new acquisition, I usually sign my contracts "As Nominee." This gives me the legal leeway to buy it in my own name, or to assign the contract to anyone else of my choosing, or an entity.

2. Since I am always trying to acquire properties with as little cash as possible, I need to make sure that I can negotiate not only a good price to buy the property, but also a good mortgage. Hence I usually put in the following clause:

> This contract is expressly subject to and conditional upon the purchaser arranging financing *suitable to himself,* such financing to be confirmed within 21 working days from the date of signing of this contract.

The words "suitable to himself" are crucial, as otherwise, if you cannot find financing on reasonable terms (such as at market interest rates), the seller may say to you that he will provide financing for the entire purchase price at 65 percent interest per annum, and since you now have financing arranged, you could be obliged to proceed with the deal.

3. Another clause I often add gives me a legal out in case we identify something is wrong with any part of the property:

> This contract is expressly subject to and conditional upon the purchaser's attorney's approval as to title, encumbrances, liens, easements, and any other regulatory impositions that may relate to the subject property, such approval to be given in writing by the purchaser's attorney to the seller's attorney by no later than 5:00 P.M. on the 20th working day after the signing of this contract.

Many standard contracts used in various parts of the world already include variations on this theme, but it pays to make sure that you are covered.

4. Depending on what you are trying to achieve and how prolific you are in a particular market, there may be advantages in having a secrecy clause in your contract, so that only the people you are negotiating with on any particular deal get to know about that deal until everything is signed, sealed, and delivered. For instance, with the downtown Phoenix commercial property that I discussed in Chapter 8, I would not necessarily want the owner or agent to know that I had successfully negotiated a great price on the transients' hotel next door, as it may alert them to what I am up to, and more important, it may cause them to raise their expectation of price on their property.

Their reasoning may be: "Wow, they got that for a song! That is going to make their deal very sweet. Surely they will still want to go ahead, even if we increase our price by half a million!" You could of course circumvent this problem by buying the high-rise building first. But in that case, you would want a secrecy clause on that deal, so that the owners of the transients' hotel didn't suddenly elevate *their* expectation of price!

When buying a single residential investment property, the need for a secrecy clause may be nonexistent. But keep it in mind. You may suddenly want to buy the three adjacent properties to meet the land requirements for putting up an apartment complex (or to sell the land to a well-heeled developer who wants to do the same). If your neighbors get wind of what you are doing, do not be surprised if the price goes up on you.

How to Make Your Offer Incredibly Seductive to the Seller

Let's assume that you have analyzed some properties, and found one to be a spectacular deal. Alone or in conjunction with your real estate agent, you have written up an offer. The offer is for less than the asking price, as you feel you can always increase your price if you want to later. Is there anything you can do to greatly increase the chances of your offer being accepted?

Well, there is. Most offers are structured such that if the seller agrees to your offer, you immediately have to come up with the deposit—a sum of money that can vary from a token amount to typically 5 percent or 10 percent of the purchase price. In other words, if the seller countersigns the contract, then you have to pay the deposit.

Staple a check for the deposit to the contract! It makes no difference to your cash flow: If they do not countersign, then they cannot bank the check, and if they do, then you would have to write it out anyway. However, the psychological power of this check stapled to the contract is phenomenal. The seller knows that you are serious. He knows that if he countersigns, he can bank the check immediately. While it doesn't make sense to me personally, I know from having applied this tactic countless times that it becomes a very persuasive element in the seller's decision as to whether or not to accept your offer.

With the cottage in Queenstown, I stapled a check for 25 percent of my offer to the contract (even so, it only amounted to $5,000). Once I stapled a check for the full offer price to the contract. The offer was not accepted (it was an ambitious offer!) but I didn't have to go up in price much before we had a deal.

On another occasion, I came across a property advertised in a real estate agency. The owner had failed to keep his mortgage commitments, and so the property was in foreclosure. Where once it had a registered appraisal of $500,000, the asking price now was $380,000.

I wrote up an offer, stapled a check with a healthy deposit to it, and handed it to the agent concerned. He took one look at the $315,000 offer figure, handed it back to me, and said that he simply couldn't submit an offer that low. I was somewhat taken aback, as I figured that agents had an obligation to submit all offers. So, I went to the head of the firm, and said: "Peter, one of us has a problem, and I don't think it's me." He asked what was going on, and I replied that I had given an offer to one of his agents, and that he had refused to submit it to the seller.

Peter replied: "Give me the offer, I will submit it personally." I handed it to him, and when he looked at the amount of the offer, his next words were: "I wish I hadn't just said that!"

Nonetheless he went around to the bank that afternoon to submit the offer. I received a phone call about an hour later. An anonymous voice with a typical banker's intonation simply said: "We have banked your check."

Stapling the check to your offer does not enhance your legal position, reduce your obligations, or guarantee the deal. But it sure makes it tempting for the seller to say yes.

It's Just a Game of Poker

Negotiating a property deal is a bit like playing poker. You may not always want to reveal why you want to buy a property, or that you already have a tenant lined up—maybe even signed up—or that you don't want this crummy old building for its own sake, but simply to use as a parking garage to enhance the value of the high-rise next door. For their part, sellers do not always want to reveal why they want to sell. They may have an ongoing dispute with the neighbors, be leaving town to be with a mistress, or be worried about the way the building shakes in earthquakes. Part of the excitement of being in real estate is that you live by your wits. If you are caught napping, you may miss an important point regarding the property you are about to buy, and not only could it cost you plenty, but there is no state-funded body to bail you out. This living by your wits has an element of excitement and adventure about it that you cannot get in many professions and occupations. And, unlike most professions and occupations, and unlike even playing poker, each time you "win a hand" at the real estate game, you increase your net worth *and* your passive income. That's no doubt why I don't care much for a profession, an occupation, or for that matter, the game of poker.

Chapter 11

GETTING HIGH ON OPIUM (AKA OPM)

> *Me:* Hey, buddy, will you lend me $50?
>
> *You:* $40? What do you want $30 for?

Generally, we are reluctant to lend people money. Nearly everyone has been burned by someone who has failed to pay back a loan. Similarly, we have all been exposed to the notion that in order to make money, you need money.

Consequently, there is something wonderfully and intuitively satisfying about making money—big dollops of it—without having to put up any capital. As we saw repeatedly in Part One, banks and other financial institutions are very willing to lend money secured against property.

In case you haven't yet got my message clearly enough, let me spell it out once again.

Banks want to give you money.
Let them give it to you!

When you buy property using Other People's Money (OPM), you are gearing your investment through leverage. You are using other people's money to make money for yourself. It almost sounds as though it should be forbidden, as though there is something alluring but illegal about it. It's as if suddenly recreational drug use is sanctioned by the government, but people are still too scared to go out and do it in public.

Well, it's perfectly legal (buying real estate with OPM, that is), and the people whose money you use even encourage you to do so!

However, just because real estate lends itself very well to using Other People's Money doesn't mean that there are no traps for novice players.

Finding Sources of Finance

A generation ago, the only viable way for most people to get a loan for a property was through a bank. Bank managers were venerated as noble pillars of society. Consequently, a visit to the bank to ask for a mortgage was a trip that most people feared. And not entirely without reason!

The bank manager would sit there, in his oversized leather chair, glaring down at you in your low chair on the other side of his huge oak desk. You would almost sit there, cap in hand, asking (begging) for him to condescend himself and the bank to consider you for a mortgage.

No wonder that even early on in my real estate investing, many friends (and friends of friends) would ask me to accompany them to the bank to ask for a mortgage. The fear from their parents' era still lingered (and I got plenty of practice at overcoming it!).

I remember reading in some magazine at that time that the biggest fear among the public was not the fear of dying, or the fear of contracting some rare and horrible disease. The biggest fear was the fear of public speaking, followed closely by the fear of asking the bank manager for a loan.

How things have changed! Today, mortgage finance is offered by many banks, financial institutions, insurance companies, contributory mortgage companies, mortgage brokers, lawyers' client funds, and even real estate companies. No longer do you have to make an appointment with the bank manager three weeks in advance! No sir, you can now call any of dozens of mortgage lenders around the clock. Many institutions even have roving "mortgage managers" who will visit you at your home, work, or investment property to offer you a deal. You can even apply for and get a mortgage on the Internet.

Of course, we now know that money is just a commodity. There is nothing special about the money from your bank. In fact, once you have the money to buy your property, it doesn't matter where the money came from. All that matters is what the terms are and the conditions associated with the loan.

At a seminar, I once heard someone say that you had to choose your bank carefully, as you didn't want your bank to go under. But what's the fear? After all, you have *their* money! At worst, the loan would be assigned to someone else.

Various Classes of Mortgages

Although a mortgage is simply an agreement to take on a loan, to pay interest on any amount outstanding, and to repay the principal according to a set plan, there are many variations on this theme, and so there are many different classes of mortgages.

The most common kind of mortgage is a *principal and interest mortgage*. Every time you make a mortgage payment, you pay interest on the amount outstanding, and some of the principal back. At the beginning of the term of the mortgage, nearly all of your payment is interest, and only a very small amount is principal. Toward the end of the term, most of the payment is principal.

An *interest-only mortgage* is where you only pay interest, until the end of the term, when you pay back all of the principal in one hit. Some mortgages even allow you to capitalize the interest: In this case, you do not pay anything for a while, and the interest payments that you would have made are instead added to the principal amount outstanding.

At the other end of the spectrum, you could borrow $300,000 today, and pay it all back tomorrow plus one day's interest.

All mortgages are simply varying ways of lending money, paying interest, and paying back principal. Which one is most suited to you (and which ones the banks will offer you) varies from time to time, country to country, and investor to investor.

Applying for a mortgage is very streamlined these days. Most banks and financial institutions have set forms to be filled out, and after much paperwork and form-signing, you have your mortgage.

For situations where things are a little more complex, a nonstandard application may help your cause.

I recommend drawing up a *proposal for finance* for each investment property you want to buy. This document will spell out exactly what it is that you *are offering* the bank, and will describe the investment property in sufficient detail for them to know that it is a safe and sound investment, both for you as investor and for them as mortgagee. A sample proposal for finance document can be found on our Web site at www.dolfderoos.com.

Of course you would include the reports from the REAP software, because then the bankers would have to agree that based on the assumptions made in the analysis, it looks like a good investment.

And when you print your proposal for finance, make eight or ten copies, and then hawk them around to various banks and lending institutions.

Many years ago, I remember the secretary of the top person at one of the nation's largest real estate companies phoned me to say that she had attended a seminar of mine some time before, and had been so enamored with what she learned that she went out and bought a property. However, even though she had done everything I had said, she was in a real bind, because her bank had turned her down. In fact, she was so distraught over this that she was almost in tears.

I asked her: "What did the other banks say?"

There was a brief silence, and then she said: "Could you repeat that?"

I said: "Sure. What did the other banks say?"

And she replied: "But I've been with this bank for fifteen years!"

I told her that I thought she had obviously been giving her bank far more loyalty than her bank was giving her, and that the only way for her to move on was to apply with many other banks. Of course, the next day she had her loan, and the new bank had *all* her business.

Getting mortgage financing is a bit of a game. Compared with even ten years ago, however, it is easy. Any good mortgage broker will guide you through the process.

Should You Pay Off the Mortgage?

One of the most difficult tasks I have is convincing people that they do not need to pay off their mortgages. In fact, I think you would be downright silly to.

Now just for the record, I am not talking about the mortgage on the home you live in, but the mortgage on your investment properties.

Why on earth would you want to pay it off?

Imagine you have a property with a mortgage of $200,000 on it. Suddenly you get hold of a lump of $50,000 in cash. It may be tax-paid income, or an inheritance from Aunt Murgatroyd, or a bonus from work. Why would you apply that $50,000 to paying down the $200,000 mortgage, when you could equally well use the $50,000 as a deposit on another $500,000 property?

What's more, by paying down the $200,000 mortgage to $150,000, you are reducing your interest payments, and therefore your tax-deductibility. While the yield on your investment property may not change (neither the purchase price nor the rental income has changed), the internal rate of return in fact goes down.

The situation gets even more bizarre if you consider that what most investors do after a number of years is refinance their properties to release some equity, to enable them to go out and buy even more property.

In other words, why use tax-paid money to pay down principal, when in doing so, not only are you reducing your tax-deductibility and therefore your internal rate of return, but you will have to pay the bank another fee to ask for your money back when you refinance?

Okay, so you may not want to use lumps of cash to pay down your mortgage. But what is wrong with having a principal and interest loan, so that, over time, the debt is paid off? There is nothing wrong with that. It's just that it may not be the smartest thing for you to do overall.

Imagine two investors, back in 1960. They each had $4,000 cash. The first used his $4,000 cash to buy one property for a purchase price of $4,000. Today it is worth, say, $250,000, and he has no debt. He has done well, but because he devoted his starting capital of $4,000 to one property, he still owns only one home.

The second investor used his $4,000 cash to buy four properties worth $4,000 each, using four deposits of $1,000 each, and four mortgages of $3,000 each. Today, his properties would be worth $1 million. If he never paid off the mortgages, he would still have a debt of $12,000, but who cares about the $12,000? It is so small (compared with the total asset value) that it almost doesn't matter.

Now let's assume further that in 1970, both investors received a lump sum of $12,000, and that by then properties had increased in value to $12,000. Our first investor, if he was lucky, may have bought another property with the $12,000 cash, so that by today he would own two for a total value of $500,00.

Our second investor had a choice: either pay off his existing debt of $12,000 on his four existing properties, or buy more property. If he pays off his debt, then he will have a cash flow advantage, but by today he would still own $1 million in property.

If, on the other hand, he used the $12,000 cash to buy more property, then he could easily have bought four more (based on the same loan-value ratio of 25 percent as with the initial properties in 1960). Thus, his $12,000 could buy him another four properties, adding $36,000 of mortgage debt to his existing $12,000. By today, he would have $2 million of property, and "only" $48,000 of debt.

It made sense for our second investor to use his $12,000 lump sum not to pay off his existing four mortgages in one hit, but to buy four more properties. Since this is true for a lump sum of $12,000, it also applies for two lump sums of $6,000, or twelve lump sums of $1,000, or 12,000 lump sums of $1.

Some Closing Thoughts on Mortgages

To give you another perspective on it, I do not buy property to own the land, as land in and of itself is nonproductive. I do not buy property to own buildings, as they deteriorate and require maintenance. I do not buy property to get tenants, as they require management. The biggest reason why I buy property is to acquire debt, for the simple reason that the amount of debt stays the same, but the asset against which that debt is secured goes up in value.

Debt on depreciating assets (such as cars, stereos, and jet skis) is bad. You shouldn't even buy these things on credit, but if you already have, pay off the debt as fast as possible. However, debt on appreciating assets is good. And as we have already seen, about the only appreciating asset for which banks are pleading with you to take on debt is property.

Furthermore, most people associate a mortgage with a problem. Wrong! When you owe the bank $5,000, you've got a problem. But when you owe the bank $5 million, *they've* got a problem!

When the numbers get that big, they have a vested interest in looking after you. So, they start to phone you to invite you to lunch. The conversation may go like this:

"Good morning, we just have had some new money come available, and were wondering if you needed any of it. How about discussing it over lunch?"

Now being as wise as you are, you realize that last week they already took you to lunch, and they paid for it, so you are wary that all this may just be a ruse to get you to buy them lunch. You are about to congratulate yourself on how astute you are when they continue:

"Of course, lunch is on us, as usual."

How can you refuse?

Once you have shown yourself to be a successful property investor, they will prefer to lend mortgage financing to you over anyone else, as they are comfortable that you will pay the interest and principal repayments. Once you have built up a portfolio, no matter how small, they will see you as serious about investing. But for someone buying his first home, or his first investment property, they perceive the risk to be much higher, as they do not know if you are a committed property owner, or a whimsical fool.

The more you play this game, the more that banks will want to give you money. I can't say it often enough: Banks want to give you money. Let them give it to you!

Chapter 12

MASSIVELY INCREASE THE VALUE OF YOUR PROPERTIES (WITHOUT SPENDING MUCH MONEY)

I n Chapter 1, I claimed that one of the attributes of property that sets it apart from other investments is that you can easily do things to property to increase its value way beyond the cost of the improvements. The possibilities are so extensive and varied, that I have devoted an entire book to detailing 101 ideas complete with examples of their implementation. However, I think it is appropriate to discuss some of them here, to give you an idea of how you can easily increase your equity with little effort or capital outlay.

The Humble Carport

One of my favorite examples of how to increase the value of a property way beyond the cost of the execution concerns a carport.

Imagine you have a residential investment property that has neither a carport nor a garage. The tenant's car must be left outside in the rain, snow, and sun.

Surely it is reasonable to assume that if you were to provide a carport with this property, the value to the tenant would go up. Now I know from experience that in many parts of Australia, New Zealand, the United States, and Canada, the additional rental that you can get by having a carport is easily around $20 per week or $80 per month. In some places it will be a bit less, and in others a bit more, but let's assume that this is a reasonable increase in rental when you put in a carport.

Now a carport is not a difficult structure to build. In essence it comprises maybe six poles with a sloping roof on top. An outlay of $1,000 generally covers it.

If you get an extra $20 per week, then your annual income from the carport will be around $1,000. In this case, the return on your $1,000 investment would be 100 percent per annum. If you owned such a residential investment property without a carport or garage, why would you not build one?

I do not know of any other investment vehicle other than property where you can easily spend an additional $1,000 and then get a massive 100 percent return on that extra investment per annum.

But our carport example doesn't stop there!

One option is to pay cash for the carport, and then receive a 100 percent return per annum. But this is how you could do even better. . . .

Imagine you had the carport built. You haven't paid for it yet, so remember that you must still pay the $1,000. However, with the new rental in place, you call the appraiser back, and tell him you want a new appraisal based on the fact that you now have increased your income by $1,000 per annum. With an extra income of $1,000, the value of the property is likely to go up by something like $10,000 (based on capitalizing the rental at 10 percent). With this new appraisal for $10,000 more, you can go back to the bank and get a new mortgage. Using a very modest 70 percent loan-value ratio, the bank will lend you $7,000 at an interest rate of, say, 10 percent.

So now you have received $7,000 from the bank. Remember, you still have to pay for the carport, so you use $1,000 of the $7,000 to pay the contractor. You also have to pay the bank annual interest of $700. (Note that the interest paid on the $7,000 mortgage may be tax-deductible only if the principal is used to generate income.) Now you are receiving an extra $1,000 per annum, so after paying your mortgage interest, you are left with only $300 of annual income.

However, you still have $6,000 left in your pocket (the $7,000 mortgage, less the $1,000 to build the carport). Ask yourself this question: Is the $6,000 taxable? Well, it certainly is not income, so no income tax is payable. And you didn't sell anything, so there can be no talk of a capital gains tax. There are in fact no tax obligations on the $6,000. This money has been created out of nothing!

Just to recap, you can either pay for your carport in cash, and receive $1,000 per year indexed for inflation (a 100 percent return on your investment of $1,000). Or, you can pay nothing, receive $300 per year indexed for inflation (an infinite return since you did not put up any capital), *and put $6,000 in your pocket on which there are no tax obligations.*

Either way, if you owned such a property, why would you not do it? And if you think that it is not worth it for a mere $1,000 per year, what if you had twenty such properties? Would you do it for $20,000 per year, or, using the second option, would you like to put $120,000 in your pocket?

Now I can already hear the "Yes, but" brigade complain in protest: "Yes, but where I come from, you couldn't possibly build a carport for a mere $1,000." Look, even if it cost you $4,000 to build, that would still represent a cash-on-cash return of 25 percent, or using the second option, you would still be putting $3,000 in your pocket. Putting no cash into the $4,000 carport is still infinitely better than putting no cash into the bank!

Let's Build Five Storage Garages

The example with the carport is real enough, but the concept also works for much larger projects. I own a block of shops that are butted up to the sidewalk, but out back there was a lot of vacant land. It was continually being overgrown by weeds, and the tenants tended to store their rubbish there. I was after a creative solution. This is what I did: I found out that rentals on storage garages were running at around $40 a week. My vacant land could just accommodate five garages, for a total of $200 per week, or just over $10,000 per year. I knew that capitalization rates on commercial properties in the area were hovering around 10 percent, so theoretically the extra rental of $10,000 per annum would increase the capital value of the property by around $100,000. All that remained to be done was to figure out what the garages would cost to build.

The quote came in at $33,000. Once again I faced a choice. Either I could build the garages for $33,000 cash and enjoy a healthy 30 percent return on capital ($10,000 annual income divided by $33,000 capital outlay), or I could have the garages built, get a new appraisal, and borrow against the extra $100,000 of equity. At 70 percent, that would put $37,000 of tax-free money in my pocket, and still give me an annual income (indexed for inflation) of around $3,000 ($10,000 rental income less, say, 10 percent interest on a $70,000 mortgage).

Again, the point is, if you are in such a situation, why would you not do it? It's not as if you have to build the carport your-self, let alone the garages. In the latter case, I simply made a se-ries of phone calls: to several contractors for quotes, to an architect for some drawings, to an appraiser to get the ap-praisal done, and to the bank to arrange a new mortgage. It is not difficult. In fact, I would go so far as to confess that it is not even particularly mentally stimulating. But it sure is lucrative!

As soon as you learn about the carport concept, I am sure that you will never see a residential investment property that does not have a carport in the same light again. In fact, when such a property is on the market, others will tend to see it in a negative light (it doesn't even have a carport!), which will fur-ther decrease interest in that property. That in turn will reduce the expectations of sale price for the seller. After a while, you will hear yourself saying: "Great!" when a property doesn't have a carport or garage.

The same applies to a property with some spare vacant land. You will wonder: "What else can I put up here that will generate income?" After all, you do not have to pay for the land!

Of course, you have to check that the carports and garages conform to local regulations in terms of site coverage (some-times, not all of the area of a property may be covered in build-ings) and other restrictions. But on average your efforts will be well rewarded.

So far, we have only covered two things you can do to mas-sively increase the value of your property without spending much money.

There are many more. You may want to do something as simple as changing all the doorknobs, to putting in a swim-ming pool. You could install an electric garage door opener, re-move old curtains, replace the carpets, install an alarm, fit vertical blinds, take out a fireplace, knock out a wall, subdivide a huge room, erect a tall fence, take down a fence, put in a skylight, seal the driveway, fit dead bolts to the doors, paint the outside, replace leaky spouting, double-glaze the windows, replace the wallpaper, and/or install a new stove. The optimal mix of improvements will depend on the state of the local market, the condition of the house in general, the specific condition of the items being considered for replacement, and the local culture.

Similar but grander things can be done with commercial properties. The biggest way to increase the value of a commercial property is, as we have seen, to acquire a property in a vacant state, and to put new tenants in. However, you can also make tremendous gains when you subdivide a large premise into smaller areas. You may not even be able to get a tenant for the original, large area, but you may fill the entire space when you rent out the smaller areas, even at a higher rate per square meter or foot. A small building on a large piece of land may not be worth much to anyone, but when you put up a high-security fence around the property, then suddenly the property is appealing to a trucking company that just needs a secure place to park its trucks at night.

Check out our Web site at www.dolfderoos.com for more details on the book *101 Ways to Massively Increase the Value of Your Real Estate Without Spending Much Money*. You can even submit ideas that we have not thought of, and look at the ideas that others have submitted.

I hope to have whetted your appetite just a little bit for the sorts of things you do to have a dramatic effect on the value of a property without spending much money.

I am hoping that if someone shouts out loud: "Property without a carport or garage!" you will immediately recognize that there is an opportunity here to put money in your pocket. In a similar vein, every time that I inspect a property, a voice inside my head blurts out all the things that I can do to massively increase the value of the property I am looking at. In that sense, when I look at a property, it is a different property from when you look at it. Of course physically it is still the same property, but we each bring with us a different set of experiences, ideas, and daring, so that a property that I think will not work for me may well work handsomely for you, and vice versa.

The secret is to do your homework, get the courage of your convictions, and then dare to try. You will either win or learn. And you never learn less.

Chapter 13

MANAGING YOUR PROPERTIES

C an you remember as a child the thrill of being told that you could get your own pet animal? Weeks of anticipation would culminate in the wonderful day when you finally received your pet. Two weeks later, however, the reality of having to feed it, wash it, groom it, and clean up after it set in. Suddenly, the notion of owning a pet was not so glamorous anymore.

Owning a property can be a bit like that. Excited as you may be about acquiring a new property, at some stage the reality of having to find new tenants, look after it, and clean it sets in.

There are consolations, though. First, unlike just about anything else you will own that requires care and attention, a property will actually feed you. Second, the whole operation can be farmed out to professional property managers. In fact you would be silly to manage your own properties as before you had acquired too many properties, this could well become a full-time job, and you would have no time (or inclination) left to find more properties.

So, while I will make a strong case later on for engaging the services of property managers wherever you own property, this chapter will start off by looking at some of the things I have learned about property management that may help you as well. These tips should help you if you decide to manage your properties yourself for a while, but they will also help you in determining whether a property management company will handle your assets in a manner that you are comfortable with.

Indeed, managing properties yourself for a while is great training to understand the components that you will want to look for in a professional property management company. By managing your own properties for a while you will gain confidence, and the knowledge to ask sensible questions of prospective managers.

Tenant Selection

About the most critical factor in running your properties smoothly is the judicious choice of tenants. With the wrong sorts of tenants, you will face a lot of trauma from late rental payments, untidy properties, high tenant turnover, excessive wear and tear, complaints from neighbors, and evictions.

Conversely, there are many things you can do to keep these sorts of problems to a minimum. Indeed, through a combination of good luck and good planning, I have managed to all but eliminate the problems that seem to plague so many investors. Let me share some of my philosophies. . . .

The most crucial determinant of the type of tenant you will attract is the area in which you buy your property. If you buy a property in the worst part of town, then the returns may be spectacular, but part of the reason why the returns are spectacular is that otherwise no buyer would be attracted there. Keep this in mind when you look at properties.

It also pays to spend a day or so interviewing prospective

tenants. Just as you have to look at 100 properties in order to end up buying one good one, you sometimes have to interview many tenants to find one that is well matched to your property.

Supply and demand comes into it too: If there is a dearth of tenants, you may be happy to accept someone that you would reject outright if there was a glut.

By interviewing many prospective tenants, you develop a nose for determining who is genuine, and who has merely borrowed the twelve-piece tweed suit to impress you during the interview.

References are useful. If the prospective tenant volunteers references, then check up on them. Phone the people involved to make sure that they are not bogus, and ask the question: "Would you have these people as tenants again?"

In jurisdictions where you can, ask the prospective tenants how long they were in their last home, what their plans are, where they are from, where their family lives, and what they do for a living. This needn't be in the form of an interrogation! Make it part of the conversation. After all, if you and I were talking, we surely would not mind sharing these details with each other. People who make good long-term tenants in general do not mind, either. If they have difficulty answering, then file that away with all the other information you are processing to make up your mind.

Another good technique is to visit the prospective tenant at their present home, if circumstances permit. I once acquired some town houses (duplexes) cheaply "off the drawing board." When they were nearly finished, I advertised for tenants in the papers, and got to speak with a Korean couple. They seemed anxious to become the tenants, as they definitely wanted to live in a new (not used) property. In fact, they were so eager that they asked me in their broken English whether I would mind showing them the rental agreement that evening. When I went around to see them, as I got to their front door, and before I even rang the doorbell, I noticed rows of shoes outside. Realizing that shoes were not permitted inside their house, I knew in that instant, before even meeting them, that I had stumbled across a conscientious couple. They were my tenants for two years, I only ever saw them once again after that initial meeting, and when they finally left the house, it was as spotless and pristine as the day they moved in.

Finding Tradesmen

There is, unfortunately, no magic formula for finding quality tradesmen. One way to increase the chances of getting good work done is to ask your friends and acquaintances if they know of a good roofing contractor, plumber, electrician, or whatever is required. Another is to join a local property investors' association (if one exists where you live) and ask for a list of recommended tradesmen.

If your friends cannot suggest anyone, and there are no references from a local property investment association, then you may have to resort to trial and error.

Once again, talk with the prospective tradesmen. Ask them if they have done that specific kind of work before, and how long they think the job will take. Then, when they have done the job, go around and check the work to see if the job was done to a standard that you are happy with.

Bear in mind that in the beginning, when you first start out investing, you will monitor the progress of every small repair or maintenance job with emotion and deep personal interest. However, as your portfolio increases in size, you will be less and less interested in the day-to-day running of the operation. If something is broken, you will simply want it fixed as soon as possible. That brings me to the next topic.

How to Get a Tradesman to Do Your Work First, Always

Whenever we need a tradesman, we generally want him instantly. I am always amused at the antics of fellow investors as they try to inspire their tradesmen to go to their properties straight away. I know of some who always allude to bigger jobs down the road if this job is done swiftly (if they weren't so busy, your "big job" may tempt them, but the reason they cannot attend to you straight away is precisely because they have so much work!). I know of one investor who tried to lure tradesmen with the promise of food and drink, again to no avail.

I have developed a foolproof method that even as I write it down seems so facile that I find it difficult to believe that it works. And yet it is so effective that I can only conclude that very few other people employ it.

The method is, simply, to pay the tradesman *the same day that you get the invoice*. Now this means that if they write out the invoice as they finish the job, then write out a check straight away. If you receive the invoice in the mail three days later, then post your check the very same day.

Word will soon spread that you always pay your account instantly. The biggest bane for tradesmen is not whether they get promises of bigger jobs down the road, or whether they get food and drink on the job, but whether they have to chase bad debtors. No one likes to phone or write debtors for money that should have been paid long ago. And yet so many people let their accounts go overdue, sometimes by days, sometimes by months, that the instant payer stands out like a breath of fresh air. Therefore, when they have a choice between two jobs, one offered by you (and they know they will have the money from that job tomorrow) and one offered by someone else (who usually pays within three or four weeks of the due date), then you can be sure that they will choose your job.

For the life of me I cannot figure out why people delay payments anyway. Most accounts accept payment "within three weeks," or "by the 20th of the month following," or "at the end of the month." What do you hope to gain by not paying for two weeks? Interest on a $2,000 bill that you manage to delay by two weeks, at an interest rate of 8 percent, is worth the princely sum of $6.15. Factor in that it is tax-deductible, and you may be looking at a saving of around $3 by delaying the payment. But that $3 will buy you a lot of goodwill, which can be priceless.

Not only does my instant-payment system get a quick response when I *need* a tradesman, sometimes they offer their services before I am even aware of a need. Once there was a violent storm in a city where I had built up a considerable property holding. Before I had even heard about the storm, the local roofing contractor called my office to ask if I had any roofs that needed repair. He put me right at the front of his queue. Like it or not, money speaks a language that everyone can understand.

Rule Enforcement

Part of the art of being a good landlord is to be firm but fair, and friendly but not familiar. Just as with any other area of business, your real skills and abilities are not put to the test so long as everything is going fine! When everything is fine, then a moron could run just about any business, including your property portfolio. It is only when there is a potential problem, such as a tenant who has skipped a rent payment, that your real worth as a manager comes into play.

The biggest mistake that I see property investors make is

trying to be too friendly with their tenants. They are immediately on a first-name basis, stop by just for chats on non-property-related topics, and generally become very familiar. I think their theory is that if they are on really good terms with their tenants, then the tenants will be more inclined to pay on time. Unfortunately, the theory can backfire.

Just as it makes sense for a property investor to assume that a tenant with whom he is friendly is unlikely to not pay the rent, so a tenant may think that a landlord with whom *he* is friendly is unlikely to take action when the payment is late. And there probably is some truth to that.

Of course, there is absolutely nothing wrong with being polite, pleasant, understanding, and compassionate. However, there is a fine line between those qualities and being a bit of a sucker and easily taken for a ride. The variations on excuses that you will come up against as to why the rent could not be paid will astound, amuse, and infuriate you. That is exactly why it pays to be firm right from day one.

Make the rent obligations that the tenant is taking on very clear. Give them a copy in writing, and talk about it during your meeting as well. More important, spell out what action will be taken if the rent is in default. And most important, if they do end up being in default, make sure you implement the appropriate action right away.

Everyone weighs the risk of breaching some rule against the consequences of getting caught *and having action taken against you.* Take parking, for instance. In my travels around the world, I come across wildly varying levels of parking fees and fines. In some cities, on-street metered parking may cost around $1 per hour, but the fine if you are caught with an expired meter is only $8. The chances of getting caught are slim: In years of parking without feeding the meter, I have only been fined once. In other cities, parking costs about the same, but if you are caught with an expired meter, the fine is $50, and if your car is still there an hour later, your car is taken away and impounded, to be released only on payment of a $400 fine. Do you think I feed those meters?

It is the same with your tenancies. If tenants know that you are fair, but that you also take swift action on any breaches of the agreement you have with them, then they will respect that, and will seek out a slower-reacting creditor to not pay when money is tight.

Accounting

The ownership of any property comes along with obligations to the tax man. Since your initial purchase is recorded on official documents, since many of your expenses are paid directly from bank accounts, and since many tenants pay by automatic bank transfers, there is so little room for "under the table" transactions that I would not even contemplate it. Apart from anything else, property has so many wonderful tax advantages that you often get money back rather than pay any taxes. Either way, you would be silly to risk something underhanded.

If you agree that you need to fully account for the dollars related to your property investment, then it only remains to be decided how you will do that. My recommendation is to have a computerized system that you update at regular intervals, such as weekly or at most monthly. This way, there will be no onerous task at the end of your financial year. On our Web site at www.dolfderoos.com, you can check out our Real Estate Management System (REMS) software. It streamlines the task of record keeping, makes filing your tax returns easy, and keeps tabs on which tenants are behind in their rent. The need for such software may not be obvious when you only have one investment property (of course Bob paid his rent for this month!), but when you have multiple tenancies, it is easy to not notice missed rent payments unless you are well organized.

Evictions

One of the toughest things you may ever need to do as a landlord is to evict a tenant. Usually this will come only after increasingly acrimonious relations with the tenant, or perhaps after a complete loss of contact with them. Either way, if it has become apparent that you are facing a losing battle in terms of getting payments from them, then it will be necessary to act quickly, decisively, and firmly.

Most countries have numerous rules regarding evictions, so make sure that you abide by them. Although it may be a tough process, you do not want to end up in a position where you are providing the tenant with free accommodation for a long time to come because you took a shortcut on some rule, wrong though that rule may seem to you.

One advantage of evicting someone is that word soon spreads like wildfire that you evict for nonpayment, and your rent collection rate will go up dramatically.

Having said all that, I have evicted only a relatively small number of tenants. Have a system in place: As soon as the rent is overdue, contact them to point it out and to remind them of their contractual obligations. It is easier to not pay someone who never calls than to not pay someone who is on the phone all the time.

Property Managers

I want you to think very carefully about something. If you own one, or two, or even half a dozen properties, it may well be possible to manage them yourself. But if you want your property portfolio to grow, so that you may end up with several million dollars' worth of property or more, do you think it is advisable—or even possible—to manage them all yourself?

My opinion is that every hour spent managing an existing property detracts from your ability to find, analyze, negotiate, finance, and own another one. Therefore, you will be wise to farm out the management to a property management company.

In Queenstown, New Zealand, apart from the $22,500 cottage that I discussed earlier, I have two other homes and a commercial property. Notwithstanding the fact that Queenstown is one of the most beautiful places in the world, and that the growth in property values can be very high, I seldom spend more than a few days a year there. Therefore, it would be folly to try to manage the properties myself.

One of the biggest advantages of having a property manager in place is that they not only do all the actual management for you (selection of new tenants, completion of the appropriate paperwork, inspections, and so on), but they also do much of the accounting. From most of my property managers in various places, I get a monthly statement detailing the gross income, the expenses incurred, their commissions, and the net amount wired into my bank account. Consequently, I only have twelve entries a year into my own accounting system, plus the depreciation issues to deal with. It makes for very easy accounting.

Typically, property managers charge anywhere from 4 percent to 15 percent of the rental income to manage your properties. Usually, the bigger your portfolio (and therefore the more desirable it is for them to manage your properties), the lower the commission rate they will settle for. This is particularly true of commercial property.

Another advantage of using property managers is that the less pleasant work of evictions, notices of rental increases, and notices requiring tenants to remedy shortcomings in keeping the property clean and tidy no longer need to be handled by you personally.

To put it another way, having a property manager enables you to work *on* your business, not *in* it.

That of course brings us to the question of how you are going to choose your property manager. Just like with the selection of a property to buy, or the selection of a real estate agent to work with, or the selection of a tradesman to work on your properties, it is somewhat of a numbers game. Go with recommendations from friends, interview prospective managers, ask them how they have dealt with particular problems in the past, and then try them. You can always change them later if you do not see eye to eye.

Further, just because you use one management company to look after one or several properties, it should not be a foregone conclusion that you always use the same firm for any subsequent properties you acquire in the same region. In fact engaging two competing firms can be healthy, in that they will each try to do well by you to win over more business.

As with any other aspect of your life, the more organized you are, the more you can take on. Develop systems to manage your properties. Even if you engage the services of property managers, develop systems to manage the managers.

As a result, you will not only benefit from Other People's Money, but also from Other People's Time.

PART THREE

Liftoff!

Chapter 14

RESIDENTIAL VERSUS COMMERCIAL PROPERTY

One of the most frequent questions I get is whether you should buy residential or commercial property. I have very strong personal views on this, but before getting to them, let's clarify just what we mean by residential and commercial property.

Classes of Property

Residential

Residential property is, as its name suggests, property that people use primarily for residential accommodation. It therefore includes freestanding homes, duplexes, condominiums, apartments, town houses, and apartment buildings. If you have an old commercial building that has been modified for residential accommodation (for instance lofts), then that is, from your perspective, a residential property investment.

Some banks classify apartment buildings as commercial property, but I want to differentiate them on the basis of whether you have residential tenants, for reasons that I explain below.

Commercial

Commercial property includes offices, shopping malls, free-standing retail shops, strip mall shops, bank buildings, medical offices, funeral parlors, restaurants, real estate outlets, pawnbrokers, coffee shops, parking lots, plant nurseries, bakeries, and convenience stores, to name just a few. If you lease out a home on a commercial lease for use as an office, then that would qualify it as a commercial property from your perspective.

Industrial

Industrial properties include warehouses, bulk-storage facilities, self-storage facilities, fuel depots, bus depots, sawmills, sewage treatment facilities, factories, power-generating plants, distribution facilities, telephone exchanges, and so forth.

Hospitality

Included in hospitality properties are hotels, motels, backpacker hostels, YWCA and YMCA hostels, youth hostels, resorts, and spas.

Despite the distinctions listed above, the term "commercial property" is sometimes used to denote all kinds of property where some form of commerce is transacted. Thus, commercial can be interpreted to include industrial and hospitality properties. Since much of what I have to say in this chapter about commercial property applies to industrial and hospitality as well, then I will simply talk about commercial property as encompassing these other two categories as well.

The Philosophical Difference Between Residential and Commercial Property

Before getting into the tangible differences between investing in residential and commercial property, let's pause to make a big distinction. When you invest in residential property, you are essentially dealing with *people*. When the rent is not paid on time, you have to deal with a person (the tenant). If you feel the property is not being kept "clean and tidy" in accordance with the rental agreement, then you will have to deal with people, who may have a different opinion as to what constitutes cleanliness and tidiness.

On the other hand, when you deal with commercial property, you are essentially dealing with *contracts*. If the rent is not paid on time, then the contract (the lease agreement) stipulates a series of remedies that the landlord can take. If the property is not kept up to a certain standard, then the contract may stipulate that you can send in a commercial cleaner and send the bill to the tenant.

Generally speaking, governments have countless rules governing the renting of property to residential tenants, which override anything that you may put in your rental agreement. For instance, in California, if tenants are behind in their rent, you can't just evict them! Bureaucrats have put all these protections in place so that the tenants will not be exploited. You have to let them fall behind in rent for thirty days before you can take action to remove them from your premises. (In contrast, when you overstay your welcome on one of their parking spots in town, they reserve the right to fine you—and in some cities impound your car—if you go even one minute over the time for which you have paid rent!) In Arizona, by contrast, the government is much more landlord-friendly, and only allows tenants to fall behind in rent for five days before you can take action.

With commercial property, on the other hand, what is in the lease contract is generally what goes.

Many commercial leases have a clause in them that stipulates that if the rent is late by more than a week, then penalty interest will be applied to the amount of rent outstanding. Furthermore, if the tenant still has not paid the rent a certain period of time after that, then you have the right not only to change the locks and take your premises back, but also to seize all the tenant's fittings, furniture, and equipment on the premises, and to sell them to recover the rent owing. Now to be sure, there are certain specific rules governing how this may be done, but the point is that your remedies as a commercial landlord are far stronger than those as a residential landlord.

When I first started out with commercial property, I used to draw up my own lease documents. This forced me to really understand each clause. Assume a tenant's rent was $9,000 per month. Then I would write up the contract to say that the rental was $10,000 per month, but subject to a discount of 10 percent if the rent was paid by the due date. Sometimes the tenants, on reading the lease, would complain that the rent agreed on was only $9,000 and not $10,000. My response would be: "But if you pay on time, it will in fact be $9,000. You do intend to pay on time, don't you?" This was a tremendous incentive to pay the rent on time.

The whole point is that with commercial property, you can (and people do) make up the rules, largely unfettered by external influences, whereas with residential property, governments the world over seem obsessed with "protecting the rights of the tenant," even when evidence shows time and time again that such protections actually work against the tenants. We will explore the interference of government in the next chapter.

As we have just discussed, with commercial property you tend to deal with contracts, whereas with residential property you tend to deal with people. Let's now explore some of the more obvious differences.

Rentals

In North America and Europe, residential rentals are quoted on a monthly basis, while in Australia and New Zealand, the default residential rental period is a week. All over the world, however, commercial rentals are quoted on an annual basis.

More particularly, with residential properties, usually the total rental figure for the property is quoted, whereas with commercial it is usually quoted *per square foot* (or per square meter). Furthermore, residential rentals are typically quoted as an all-inclusive figure, whereas commercial rentals are quoted as so much per square foot *plus costs* (where costs include things like insurance and property taxes).

Care of the Property

With commercial property, the tenants usually derive their income at your premises. Thus, particularly if their clients visit them at the premises, they have a vested interest in keeping the property looking good. With residential tenants, there is not the same drive to maintain your property, let alone improve it.

Over the years I have noticed that all of my commercial tenants tended to improve their properties, sometimes without even consulting me, and sometimes, as most of my lease contracts specify, by getting my consent first. Remember the woman who turned the butcher shop into a delicatessen? She spent over $30,000 renovating the premises (replacing the old concrete cool-store with a modern one, replacing walls, putting in a new floor, among other improvements). These things are still in my building, even though she has long since sold her business to someone else (who has since also sold it). But my building still has the benefit of her remodeling work. Remember the funeral parlor operator? He spent some $25,000 putting shutters on all the windows, extensively remodeling the inside, and putting in decorative gardens. He too has since left, but his work remains behind.

Contrast that with my residential tenants. As I sit here I am thinking hard to recall even one instance where a residential tenant has improved one of my properties, but I cannot think of anything. Furthermore, none of my residential tenancy agreements mention anything about how improvements will be accounted for (financially), which shows it is not a common occurrence. However, my commercial leases tend to have a clause which stipulates that tenants may only make additions, alterations, or improvements with the approval of the landlord, and furthermore that if the landlord is to pay for any improvements, then the tenant will pay a percentage of the improvement cost as increased rental. The prevalence of this clause in one form or another shows that improvements are common with commercial property.

In conclusion, commercial tenants want to improve their

(your!) property all the time, whereas residential tenants do not really care.

Some of my commercial tenants paint their premises every two years, not because they want to please me, but for their own reasons. More important, if a tap leaks in one of my commercial properties, the tenant tends to either fix it, or have it fixed by someone fast: They earn their income there and want to get on with the job at hand. With residential properties, on the other hand, even if the tenants have the skills and tools to make minor repairs, the psychology of renting houses is that you call the landlord if anything happens.

In other words, I get far fewer calls to fix and repair things on my commercial properties than I do on residential.

Lease Length

Another fundamental difference between residential and commercial property concerns the typical length of the contracted lease period.

With residential properties, it is slowly becoming more popular to have six-month contracts or even one-year contracts. But in many places, residential properties are still rented out on a month-to-month basis.

Commercial properties, on the other hand, are generally leased out for many years at a time. On smaller strip mall–style shops, the rental period may only be for periods of two years at a time. But on larger buildings, the leases may run for many years—leases of twenty years are not uncommon.

With residential properties, from a tenant's perspective, a long lease is seen as an imposition, as something that reduces your freedom to move on if you so desire. After all, if you pay the rent on time, your landlord is unlikely to want to evict you, so why sign up for a long time?

With commercial property, on the other hand, a long lease is generally seen as something desirable from even the tenant's perspective—it gives their company or business the security of the same premises to operate out of. In fact, many tenants of mine, as their lease draws to an end (or sometimes years before), ask me for a new, longer lease, or an extension on an existing lease. This may sound absurd initially, but consider a tenant who wants to sell his business. He will not get much for it if the lease only has seven months to run and he cannot guarantee that you as landlord will extend the lease for the new tenant. Part of the value of any business is the goodwill factor of clients knowing where the business is, and going there regularly. To be sure to maintain that goodwill, many tenants will seek out long-term leases. Banks obviously like long-term leases as well: The longer and stronger the lease, the more willing they are to lend money on the property.

Getting a New Tenant

With residential property, if a tenant leaves, that is usually the end of your association with that tenant. Certainly, if a new tenant fails to pay the rent, you cannot go back to the previous one and ask him for the shortfall! And yet that can happen with commercial property.

When a business is sold, it is not as if the existing lease comes to an end, to be replaced with a new one for the new tenant. Rather, an assignment of lease document is executed, which means that the lease is assigned or transferred to the new tenant. Clauses in this document stipulate that should the new tenant fail to meet its obligations, then the previous tenant is still there as guarantor to the new tenant. Part of the reason for this is to prevent a tenant who wants to quit his business from selling it to anyone at random and thereby absolving himself of any lease responsibilities. Without such a clause, few landlords would ever sanction the sale of a business. Of course when the lease comes up for renewal, then only the incumbent tenant will sign (the previous tenants are not required to stay on the new lease, and would be foolish to do so).

Sometimes, a business operated in one of my properties may have had three or four assignments of lease during the term of the lease. I do not mind at all: I then have three safety nets to ensure that the rent will be paid.

Finding a New Tenant

So far there have been a lot of advantages of commercial properties. Not all the advantages are stacked in the favor of commercial property, though.

The biggest advantage of residential property over commercial comes when your property is empty. If you have a house where the tenants have just left, then it should be relatively easy to find new tenants. If it has been empty for three weeks and you are starting to despair, then do not fret! The house is not empty because the carpet in the living room is the wrong color, or because the bedroom is facing the wrong way, or because the window in the dining room is too high. There is only one reason why the house is still empty: The rental is too high relative to market rental in that area at that particular time. Drop the rent by 5 percent or maybe 10 percent and you will get a tenant.

On the other hand, if you have a commercial property that has been empty for three months or even three years, then the problem may not be that the rent is too high. Even if you were to slash it in half or more, you may still not find a tenant.

The reason for this difference is simple. Just about any residential property on the market has all that is required for someone to live in it. It will have at least one bedroom, a kitchen, a bathroom, and so on. In other words, we all tend to agree on what is needed in a residential property to make it functional as a home, and therefore anyone could, if needed, live there. However, when it comes to commercial property, how do we stipulate what is required? The requirements vary wildly from commercial tenant to tenant. Hence, when a tomato cannery becomes vacant, it may not simply be a matter of reducing the rent to find a tenant. No matter how much you drop the rent, no photographer looking for a studio is likely to settle for the tomato cannery. No wine bar operator is likely to want a mini-storage facility, and no shoe store that largely relies on passing foot traffic will want the top floor in an office tower, no matter how good the view or cheap the rent.

Commercial property is far more specialized than residential, and hence it may be more difficult to find a tenant in the areas of specialization catered to by your premises.

Capital Required to Buy

There is a general notion that in order to buy a commercial property, you have to be a very wealthy person, while more modest means will suffice to buy a residential property. While in general this may be true, we have already seen in Chapter 8 that it is possible to buy a viable commercial property for $59,000 that has all the advantages of any commercial property. So long as people think that commercial properties are expensive, then you will have little competition looking at small (low capital value) commercial buildings.

To the extent that it is true that commercial properties are generally more expensive than residential properties, there is a commensurate benefit. To own $10 million worth of residential property, you generally would have to own a lot of separate properties, with many dozens of separate rental agreements. The management overheads could be huge! A single commercial property, on the other hand, could be worth the same $10 million. You may have only one lease document, and therefore much reduced management concerns.

Since there are so many people in the market for a residential property, and since the capital values involved tend to be much smaller, it will be much more difficult to find a residential property selling for less than 10 percent of its replacement cost than a commercial property at such a discount.

Let me give you an example. In the mid-1990s I was involved in a bid on a building in downtown Dallas, Texas, known as the Republic Tower. It actually comprised three towers of fifty floors, thirty-three floors, and eight floors respectively. When the first tower was built, it was the tallest building west of the Mississippi. The revolving searchlight on top could be seen at night for many miles. The buildings comprised a massive 1.92 million square feet of rentable space. The cost to replace the buildings was around $300 million. What would you have offered for these buildings?

My consortium's offer was in fact for $15 million. That is not a typo! We were offering around 5 percent of the cost of replacing the buildings.

Now at this stage I should give you a few more details. Commercial buildings are generally valued on the basis of their rental income. The Republic Tower back then was only around 6 percent leased. In fact, the total rental income did not cover the operating expenses: There was a shortfall of $1.6 million. Based on a capitalization rate of around 10 percent for office space, that would have put a value on the property of *negative* $16 million.

On the other hand, with market rentals of around $20 per square foot (per annum), the building had a potential rental income of nearly $40 million per year (1.92 million square feet times $20 per square foot). At that same capitalization rate of 10 percent, that would give it a value of almost $400 million.

Now for a number of reasons, our bid was not successful. In case you are thinking: "I should think not! I don't want to hear of anyone buying well over $300 million worth of property for $15 million in one fell swoop," then take heart. In December of 1997, the property was reportedly sold to a partnership involving Credit Suisse First Boston for the princely sum of $25 million. They are now spending $75 million completely refurbishing the property (including, for instance, replacing all of the 8,000 panes of glass with dual-pane, energy-efficient reflective glass). But even so, it is a great deal, and a testament to my strategy that you can find properties that are selling for a fraction of their real value, if only you are willing to look for the extraordinary, for properties with a twist, for properties where by changing something around, you can reap huge benefits.

Another deal I was involved with concerned a massive single-story building in the Sydney suburb of Yennora. Known as the Sydney Wool Exchange, this building comprised a vast three million square feet of warehouse space. It was believed to be the largest building in the Southern Hemisphere, and it took quite some time just to *drive* around the perimeter. The wool clipped from some 20 million Australian sheep would pass through its storage facilities. The building was built for the government, owned by the government, and leased to the government. And now, the government had decided it was time to sell.

Since the rental income was $7.9 million, and since capital-ization rates were around 11 percent, it was determined through initial negotiations that a sale might be effected at around $72 million.

On the face of it, a return of 11 percent would not get me excited at all. However, there were some extenuating circumstances.

First, by only considering the capitalized income, you are completely overlooking the fact that the three-million-square-foot building was sitting on seven million square feet of land. The government had not taken the land value into account, probably on the basis that it was not generating any income anyway. The surplus land was worth some $16 mil-lion, however.

Second and far more important, the government, as we have noted, was leasing this building to themselves. In other words it was money out of one pocket and into another. They had no vested interest in getting a market rental for the build-ing, as it would not benefit them anyway. The average rental of some $2.63 per square foot was nowhere near market rentals. The large, national tenant in the building next door was paying $5.60 per square foot, more than double.

We commissioned an appraisal, which came in at over $140 million. In the end, we were outbid by a consortium from Hong Kong, who bid $2 million more than we did, but they still got it at effectively half price. The point is, these deals exist! In this case there was over $60 million to be made after costs.

In mentioning these examples, I am not trying to impress you with big numbers, but rather trying to impress upon you that great deals happen all the time, from little $22,500 cot-tages and $59,000 commercial buildings, right through to com-mercial properties worth many hundreds of millions of dollars. And by the way, the effort involved in buying a $1 million building is about the same as the effort involved in buying a $100 million building. Would you rather do a $100 million deal once, or a $1 million deal 100 times?

Loan-Value Ratios Available

Banks and financial institutions will easily lend you 80 percent of the value of a home. Some readily go to 90 percent, and depending on economic circumstances, some even go to 100 percent and above.

Such high loan-value ratios, however, are extremely uncommon with commercial properties. Typically, banks will lend 50 percent of the appraised value of a commercial property. Some will go to 60 percent, and more rarely you can talk banks into 66 percent.

Having said that, it is generally much easier to instantly increase the value of a commercial property from the low purchase price you paid to the new appraised value after you have owned the property for a few weeks. The reason is simply that an empty residential property still appraises for close to what its value would be if it were occupied. However, an empty commercial building is not worth much at all.

Consequently, you may buy a commercial property for a song, put in a tenant that you had lined up before you bought the property, get a new appraisal, go to a bank, get a modest 50 percent mortgage, and still end up with more money than you need to pay for the property according to the contract price. I did a similar thing with the funeral parlor described earlier. You may recall I bought it for $170,000. That is probably all that it was worth empty. However, with tenants installed paying $30,500 per annum, even the bank thought it was worth at least $240,000. My 66 percent mortgage of $160,000 *almost* covered the purchase price. These things are easier to do with commercial properties than with residential properties.

Management Overheads

The nature of residential properties is such that once you get to own about twenty of them, you almost have a full-time job looking after them. Of course weeks may go by where you have hardly any phone calls, late rent payments, or maintenance requirements to sort out. By the same token, during some weeks you may be working overtime.

Commercial properties on the other hand are not nearly as demanding of your time. As we have seen, tenants tend to look after minor repairs themselves. Tenant turnover is not nearly as high, and is very predictable—just look on your lease schedule to see when the leases come up for renewal. When you have many tenants in one building, one watertight roof means many tenancies with no leaking roof problems (compare that with residential properties, where twenty tenants in separate homes means twenty roofs to maintain).

The difference in management overheads can be highlighted in another way: Whereas all of my residential properties are managed by professional managers, many of my commercial properties are not managed by outsiders at all. These properties attract so few phone calls per year, have so few maintenance and upkeep requirements, and have such low tenant turnover, that it does not seem cost effective to me to give up 10 percent or even 5 percent of the rent roll to have someone else handle the few calls and management issues during the year.

Here is a summary of the differences between residential and commercial property.

Residential Versus Commercial Property

Residential	Commercial
Rentals are quoted monthly or weekly.	Rentals are quoted annually.
Tenants have little interest in maintaining or improving the property.	Tenants have a strong vested interest in keeping the property looking good and functional, and even improving it.
Leases are nonexistent or tend to be short.	Leases tend to be long.
Tenants phone you for minor problems.	Tenants tend to fix minor problems.
Bureaucrats tend to stick their noses in protecting the rights of the tenant.	Bureaucrats tend to leave you alone.
Capital required to buy can be minimal.	Capital required to buy can be large.
Banks will easily lend up to 90 percent and more of appraisal.	Banks will lend only 50 percent to 60 percent of appraisal.
Appraised value when empty is not much less than when tenanted.	Appraised value when tenanted may be two or three times the value when empty.
If the property is empty, it is usually easy to find a new tenant.	If the property is empty, it may be difficult to find a new tenant.
For a large sum invested, the management overhead can be high.	For a large sum invested, the management overhead is usually low.
You deal with people.	You deal with contracts.

Residential or Commercial— Which Is Right for You?

Whether you should invest in residential property or commercial property is a decision that you will have to make on your own. I do have some points to offer for your consideration, though.

If real estate seems daunting to a lot of people starting out in the game, then commercial property is far more daunting than residential. The reason is simply that everyone knows what constitutes a home that someone could live in. You would notice the absence of a kitchen, or a bathroom, or if there were no windows!

However, if you came across a commercial property with no kitchen, no bathroom, or no windows, would that matter? Storage units would be worth *less* if they had windows (as then people could see what you were storing, and the risk of theft or arson would be greater). So it is much more difficult for beginners to know what it is that commercial tenants will want. Whereas residential properties tend to have a lot in common, commercial properties are far more specialized.

Having said that, if you are serious about having a growing portfolio, then for me I would rather have a large amount of money tied up in commercial property than in residential property. Imagine if you wanted $20 million worth of properties. That would be a lot of homes, with a lot of plumbing, roofs, gardens, and wiring to maintain! On the other hand, a commercial portfolio of $20 million may comprise just a few properties, with much less management overhead. Furthermore, the tenants of commercial properties tend to pay the outgoings (property taxes, insurance, maintenance, and so on), they have a vested interest in keeping the properties looking good, there is much less government interference, they have signed up on long-term leases, you as landlord have stronger remedies if the rent is not paid, and since the tenants derive their income there, the chances of having defaulting tenants is in my experience much less.

The reasons I have just outlined may help explain why, of all the extremely high-net-worth property investors I know, only two own predominantly residential properties. The rest all own commercial.

Chapter 15

GOVERNMENT INTERFERENCE

I t will come as a surprise to many people that the property market is in fact the largest industry in just about every Western nation. When you consider the capital tied up in property, and the annual rental values, then the size of the property industry exceeds the next biggest industry by a wide margin.

The fact that the property market works so efficiently is a testament to the natural forces of supply and demand largely unfettered by the interference of governments. I believe that property markets are the biggest and most free markets anywhere in the world. Other markets, such as those for commodities, stocks, futures, and options, are highly regulated and controlled. Real estate on the other hand is mostly left to the natural forces of supply and demand.

There are some notable exceptions, however, that make an interesting exercise in showing how, more often than not, the effect of government intervention is exactly the direct opposite of that intended.

Let me give you an example. At various times, governments have deemed it necessary to impose rent-rise restrictions to protect innocent tenants from the greedy claws of rapacious landlords.

On the surface such restrictions sound perfectly justifiable. Assume that for whatever reason, there is a sudden shortage of accommodation, and that landlords capitalize on the situation by increasing the rent on their properties to way above what the market "should be." Tales of suffering of particular tenants are reported on the news, and before you know it, politicians are on their soapboxes promoting the imposition of rental controls so that landlords cannot increase their rentals "on a whim." Needless to say, the theory is well received, as which good citizen with a conscience would want these tenants to suffer at the hands of the rapacious landlords?

A law is passed, limiting the increase in rent that a landlord may impose to the annual inflation rate, or to the consumer price index. So far so good.

But before long there is a problem. Sometimes, property values (and therefore rental levels) rise more slowly than the general inflation rate, and sometimes they rise faster. Let's assume that property prices have doubled in a relatively short time (because of the same forces of supply and demand that would have caused rents to rise), but that rentals, restricted to the inflation rate, have only gone up by 5 percent. Suddenly, the yields on rental properties have almost halved. The natural effect is that fewer investors will want to invest in property in that region, and many existing investors will sell and get out. Consequently, the pool of available rental stock will diminish. Through the forces of supply and demand, the price of rental accommodation would be driven up even further, but because of the rent-rise restrictions, the few available are held artificially cheap. A black market may develop, people become reluctant to move (because then landlords can impose a new, "market" rental), and the spiral continues. With more investors leaving the market, rental prices rise even further.

The net result is the *exact opposite* of that intended by introducing the rent-rise restrictions in the first place. The best thing for governments to do when rentals rise steeply is sit back and do nothing, as then, again through supply and demand, developers will build new housing stock until rentals come back down to an equilibrium.

This phenomenon is real. The Netherlands introduced rent-rise restrictions soon after the Second World War. An aunt of mine in The Hague lived in the same apartment for forty years because her rent was the equivalent of around $38 a month, and the day she moved, she would have had to pay market rentals somewhere else that would have been orders of magnitude higher. Since rentals were kept *artificially* low by the rent-rise restrictions, yields were artificially low, and therefore developers had no incentive to build new stock. Is it any wonder that the Netherlands had a housing shortage long after Germany did, even though a much greater proportion of Germany's housing stock had to be replaced?

In New Zealand in the mid-1970s, the flamboyant prime minister at the time, the late Sir Robert Muldoon, introduced not just a rent restriction, but a rent (and wages) *freeze*. The net effect was a chronic shortage of rental accommodation, and prices that, when the rent freeze was finally and inevitably lifted, went sky-high.

In the United States, the city with some of the highest rentals in the country, San Francisco, is also the city with the harshest rent-rise restrictions.

My point in raising this whole issue is as follows. The reason why property works so well as an investment vehicle all over the world is largely because it is self-directed and self-regulated through the natural forces of supply and demand. The minimal government interference that there is (through rent-rise restrictions and absurd and onerous obligations imposed on landlords to be forgiving of defaulting residential tenants) hinders rather than helps the very people that the interference is designed to protect.

It is incumbent on all of us to be aware of what local and national politicians are trying to impose, to think it through, discuss it, and to do our bit to ensure that the market is kept alive, pure, and functional. This is not just self-serving; it also helps tenants, the very body of people that the government purports to be protecting at our expense.

Chapter 16

THE EIGHT GOLDEN RULES OF PROPERTY

The reasonable person accepts the world the way it is.
The unreasonable person insists on changing the
world to suit his own requirements. That is why all
progress depends upon the unreasonable person.

Investing in real estate is definitely infectious. You either love it, or you don't. If you don't, you can't fake it, and if you do, you can't hide it.

Recently, I was sitting at a table with a friend discussing some business when, seemingly mid-sentence, he said: "How would you like to look at some properties?" At first I wasn't quite sure whether he meant figuratively or literally, but I replied: "Always!" Within minutes we were in the truck cruising around Phoenix, phoning agents who had "For Sale" signs up, discussing rental trends, and looking for "angles."

If driving around town looking at properties is a chore to you, then property is probably not for you. But if you can be perfectly happy cruising around looking for great deals, then you have the makings of a devout property investor.

Over the years, I have been lucky enough to meet many accomplished investors, and to have read even more books on the subject. From what they taught me, and my own experiences, I want to leave you with my Eight Golden Rules of Property. These rules may not be the "be-all and end-all" of property. There are many other things to take into consideration when investing in property. But when these eight rules are followed, success will be close by.

1. You make your money when you buy.

Even though we have said that property is very forgiving of mistakes, you make the huge dollops of profit by buying well at the beginning. When you buy a $240,000 property for a mere $165,000, then whichever way you look at it, you have just made $75,000 tax-free. It may not be in the form of folding cash, but it is $75,000 that you can add to your net worth nonetheless. It can take a long time to earn that same $75,000 from a job, or even as surplus income over expenses from a property. Keep looking, and you will keep on finding great deals.

2. Always buy from a motivated seller.

If you ask someone whether or not his property is for sale, and he replies, "No way, I love this property and never want to move, although if you pay me enough, I will of course consider it," then you are unlikely to buy that property at a cheap price. The more motivated (read desperate!) the seller, the better the deal will be for you. And don't feel guilty that you are buying it for what seems like a steal: You are still paying him more than his next best offer, right?

3. Fall in love with the deal, not the property.

One of the biggest mistakes I see investors make is when they buy an investment property not on the basis of the returns, but because they "absolutely adore that cute little property." There is nothing wrong with adoring a property. In fact, when it comes to choosing a home to live in, the more you like the property, the happier you are likely to be. But when it comes to an investment property, leave your emotions behind. You are building passive investment income. Stick to investment factors: Do the numbers work? What are the growth prospects? It is a numbers game. There is nothing adorable about a funeral parlor.

4. Never be the first to name a figure—that person always loses.

During my weekend Property Investor Schools, I get the students to play a negotiation game. I split the group into buyers and sellers of imaginary properties. I tell the buyers what a property is appraised at, and what they are willing to pay for it. I then tell the sellers the same appraised value, and what they need to sell it for. Then I let them loose on each other. The results are hilarious. In all cases, the buyer-seller pairs are negotiating the same property, with the same known, appraised value. Buyers never pay more than the maximum I specify, and sellers never sell for less than the minimum I specify. And yet, a particular property may be transacted at, say, anywhere from $380,000 to $690,000. There are many lessons to come out of this game (especially if you are in it, rather than reading about it), but the first and most glaringly obvious is that the first person to name a figure nearly always loses. Even those negotiators who think they did a good deal often cringe when they hear what a rival buyer (or seller) did the same deal at.

This rule of never being the first to name a figure works in all aspects of your life, and not just property. It will just be worth a lot more to you in your property dealings than when negotiating at the local yard sale!

5. Be countercyclical.

It takes a lot of fortitude to go against the grain. And yet to do well in property, you have to cultivate the stamina to do just that: to buy when everyone else is selling, and to bide your time when everyone else is buying.

In the early 1980s in New Zealand, tight monetary conditions resulted in mortgage interest rates going through the roof: They were over 20 percent per annum. People were telling me I was crazy to be in property. Even when I tried to finance a wooden villa (split into two apartments) with two newer rental units at the rear of the property, the banks asked me if I was sure I wanted to proceed, given that interest rates were so high. In the end, there was only one bank who would even lend me the money, a bank called Broadbank, and the interest rate was a whopping 24 percent per annum. Why did I still proceed? Well, first off, my yield was 27 percent, so my interest was covered, but more important, I knew that as interest rates fell (which had to happen sooner or later), then property prices would skyrocket, as the prices of properties were based on affordability. And that is exactly what happened: Within a year, interest rates were back in the low teens, and the value of the property took off. (Just as a point of interest, Broadbank is no longer around but the villa with the two units still is.)

Similarly, when there is a boom on, when everyone is jumping in thinking that there will be no end to the increases in price, that is when you should lie low. Conversely, when everyone else is trying desperately to get out, that is when you must have the fortitude to go in there, boots and all, and buy as much as you possibly can. People's memory is very short. For a while after the 1987 stock market crash, the masses vowed never to risk all on the market again. But a mere ten years later, an unprecedented amount *and proportion* of Americans' net worth was invested in the market. Sometimes it is not easy to know if a market is at a peak or merely climbing, or if it is at the bottom or still falling. (Remember, I did not hear many people say in early October of 1987 "Sell! Get out! The market is at its peak!") Therefore you sometimes have to make a judgment call. But with property you can generally tell when a market is low. Advertisements tend to state things like: "Any offer considered," "Vendor financing available," "Come and make a deal," "Settlement terms to suit the buyer." Properties are on the market for a long time. As a buyer, you are welcomed with open arms by both real estate agents and the owners of properties that you are inspecting. For you, these times are great.

6. Always try to buy with zero or little down.

For years we have been told by our parents to "pay off your debt." There is something unnerving about having a big mortgage. We have this natural inclination to want to get rid of it. Consequently, when it comes to buying property, we tend to want to put in as much cash as we can.

And yet putting in a lot of cash does not make good investment sense. Remember from Part One of this book how one of the biggest advantages of investing in real estate is that you do not need to put up all of the money yourself? Well, the less money you put up, the bigger the advantage to you. First, your returns will be higher (not the yield, but certainly the cash-on-cash return and the internal rate of return). Second, you will be able to buy more properties. Instead of spending $100,000 cash on a single property costing $100,000, why not put down a $25,000 deposit on each of four $100,000 properties, or even a $10,000 deposit on each of ten $100,000 properties?

7. Seldom Sell.

It is tempting for me to write: "Never Sell." In general, people who sell their properties (to cash in on the lure of a profit) never do as well as people who just keep hanging on to their properties. When you talk with people who owned properties in the past, they will visibly cringe when you ask them what those properties would be worth today. I have heard more often than I can remember, retired people telling me that the house they bought back in 1962 for, say, $4,200 is now worth $365,000, *and how they wish that they had only bought two of them.* Imagine if they would have bought ten!

Now I realize that sometimes circumstances force you to sell, or make it wise to sell. One day, the restaurant in Cass Bay I described in Chapter 10, after years of having a succession of tenants, was vacant. As such, its value plummeted. Then I got a call from Switzerland: Someone wanted to run it as a restaurant, but decided that the only circumstances under which they would do so would be if I would sell them the property. Now I may believe in the general concept of never selling, but I am not silly!

Sometimes it is wise to sell. Occasionally you may have to cut your losses, or quit a property that is draining a greater than normal proportion of your resources (financial, staff, or mental energy). However, in general, people who hang on to properties for decades thank their lucky stars that they did, and people who sell, apart from having to think of taxes such as capital gains tax and depreciation recapture tax, one day see the property at the new, current market price, and are forced to think: "Wow, I could have still owned that property and made an extra million or two for no extra work."

8. The Deal of the Decade comes along about once a week.

I have kept the most important rule until last. As I have alluded to at the beginning of this book, if you believe that great deals do not really happen, then you will not see one even if you fall over it, or if someone hands it to you on a silver platter. Of course, the more good deals you see, the more you will believe they exist. If you are just beginning and not yet a believer, then the only way out of this impasse is to start looking, and keep looking. You will be amazed at what you will find.

Years ago, when a girlfriend of mine had her birthday, I told her that I had hidden her present somewhere in the house. She got very excited as she started searching for it. Eventually of course she found it, and she thanked me profusely. After breakfast, I told her that I hadn't just hidden one present in the house, but three. Once again, she got very excited, and started looking again until she had found all three. Once again, she thanked me profusely.

After lunch, I told her that to tell the complete story, I had to reveal that there were in fact ten presents hidden throughout the house. Once more, she got very excited, and resumed her search. However, as each present became more and more difficult for her to find (and I couldn't know when I hid them which ones would be easy and which would be difficult), it took her longer and longer.

However, knowing they were there, she persevered, until she found all ten. Needless to say, she thanked me again profusely.

But you see, she didn't start looking for the first present until after I had told her that I had hidden one. She stopped looking when she had found it, because she had no reason to believe that there would be any more. It was only when I told her there were three that she continued her search. Similarly, when she found the first three, she stopped looking again, as she had no reason to suspect that there may be any more. Even when she had found all ten, she stopped looking, even though she might have had reason to suspect (falsely, as it turns out) that I may have hidden even more.

When it comes to real estate, the problem is that there is nobody to tell us how many good deals there are out there that we should be looking for. And just like my girlfriend, we tend to not look unless we know for sure that something is there.

It takes a certain courage to look for something, risking all along that you may not find it. If you refuse a friend's invitation to go out sailing because, so you say, you are "looking for a $22,500 cottage worth much more, or a $59,000 commercial property worth $100,000, or a $400 million office tower for a mere $15 million," then they are likely to think you are a bit crazy. But when you find them, you can not only go out sailing, you can go out and buy a boat or two.

If you truly believe that the Deal of the Decade comes along about once a week, then just as surely as my girlfriend found her presents, you will find your deals.

Chapter 17

THE WORLD IS YOUR OYSTER

Laugh and the world smiles with you.
Sleep, and you snore alone.

When I was a child, I used to play the game Monopoly for hours at a time with my friend Dean. However, after a while, the board that came with the game was too small, too repetitive, and too boring for us.

So we created our own board. We unfolded large cardboard boxes, laid them out flat in the huge living room of Dean's family farmhouse, and created our own board with felt-tip pens, inventing our own stations to charge rent on should the other be unlucky enough to land on it. We also ditched the little plastic progress markers that came with the game for far more stylish Matchbox Lamborghinis and Porsches.

While writing this book, it suddenly occurred to me that I hadn't played Monopoly in literally decades. I wondered why, and while I was having fond memories of turning the living room at Dean's house into a vast real estate empire, it suddenly dawned on me. I haven't played Monopoly in decades on a board because my life has become one huge game of Monopoly. *I play the game every day.*

There are, to be sure, some differences between the Monopoly of Dean's living room and the Monopoly of my life that are worth noting. One is that you win the game of Monopoly by bankrupting your opponents (your friends, for heaven's sake!). In real life, you can "collect the rent" from people who, at best, willingly pay it in return for accommodation or premises to run their businesses from, and at worst from people who acknowledge that if they weren't paying rent to you, they'd be paying it to another landlord.

Another difference is that in the game of Monopoly, you collect money only when someone (unwillingly!) lands on one of your properties. In my real-life Monopoly, I do not have to wait for someone to chance upon my properties for one rent payment at a time: I have signed most of them up on long-term leases. What is more, they do not land there unwillingly. Every tenant I have taken on leases or rents my premises by choice. They may not relish paying rent, but they choose to rent there nonetheless.

What is more, I can play my real-life game of Monopoly all over the world. Real estate is truly international. With many professions such as doctor, attorney, dentist, psychiatrist, and pilot, if you want to practice in a new country, you have to study again and pass examinations to prove you are qualified for the local conditions. Even if you want to be a real estate agent, you have to gain local qualifications.

But if you want to be an investor, there are no qualifications required! You can move around from country to country, picking the eyes out of local conditions, rules, tax laws, and economic circumstances. Unlike many other professions, there are no stand-down periods, no minimum-stay requirements, no residency requirements, and no qualification requirements. For instance, there is nothing to stop you from spending two weeks looking at investments in Czechoslovakia, one week in Italy, and then a month in Finland, if that is what took your fancy. Most professions would find such liberty impossible.

Furthermore, you do not even need the money to invest. If you want to invest in most other asset classes, a normal question would be (and is): "How much money do you have to invest?" But in all my years of investing in real estate, I have never been asked how much money I have. Occasionally I will be asked: "What price bracket are you looking in?" Now, you can say anything you like. My normal response is that price is not as important as the returns, or the nature of the twist in the property. Who cares if the purchase price is three times what I have in the bank? I can find someone else to put up the money! Remember, banks want to lend you money to buy property!

Given that investing in property is so relatively simple and so uniform around the world (there are few local rules to learn), and that it is so easy and cheap to travel these days, I am utterly surprised that most people still only consider owning investment properties within a few miles of their home. What is stopping them from finding real estate gold mines further afield? (Mind you, it surprises me that the vast majority of people die within a few score miles of where they were born, and that the majority of people when they retire cannot put their hands on $12,000 despite working for an entire career.) Of course some countries like Japan make it exceedingly difficult for foreigners to invest in their country. But there are many countries where there are no or minimal restrictions.

Imagine I told you that there was a Western country where there was no capital gains tax, no estate or death taxes, no wealth tax, no transfer tax or stamp duty, unlimited deductibility of losses (paper or real) in one enterprise against profits in another, no limit to the amount of mortgage interest you can deduct against income, and generous depreciation rates based on purchase price and not written-down book value as passed on from owner to owner. Would this pique your interest? What if I went on to say that capital growth in this country had averaged 10 percent per annum for the last 100 years, that there was a stable political environment, and that the country in question was an extremely desirable place to live. Would you think of going there to invest?

Such a country exists! It is New Zealand. What if you went there for two weeks and didn't find an investment property that met your criteria? Would that have been two weeks of your life utterly wasted? Of course not! Hopefully, you would have had some fun, learned a bit, met some interesting people, and gained some knowledge in property that will make your next scouting trip—to New Zealand or anywhere else—more likely to succeed. And such a trip, being part of your business as an investor, would be tax-deductible.

Does this mean that all New Zealanders only ever invest in New Zealand? Of course not! Many New Zealanders invest on the Gold Coast of Australia. Why would they do that, given that in Australia there is a capital gains tax, there is a stamp duty or transfer tax, the written-down book value of a property is passed on from owner to owner for depreciation purposes, and marginal tax rates are much higher?

Perhaps it is for the lure of the Gold Coast, the dream of maybe retiring there one day to enjoy the fine weather, the expected high growth brought on by the population influx, and the sheer adventure of going somewhere else and having the whole exercise tax-deductible since it is what you do for a living. The point is, anyone can invest almost anywhere.

There is no one optimal place to invest. That means that your suburb in the city where you live is not the only place that you should consider. Open your mind to the possibilities. There are always windows of opportunity that come up from time to time. Since the Berlin Wall came down in 1989, we have seen some spectacular opportunities come and go. I have just been to Eastern Europe. Right now the prospects for Prague and Budapest are tremendous. Who knows where the next great opportunities will be. But by sitting at home watching the local newscast to see which crimes have been committed, you will no more hone your international investment skills, let alone increase your passive income, than wake up on the moon.

We are going to be dead for a mighty long time. Every moment counts. Make the most of life. Decide what it is you want to do, and then go out there and do it. If you are not having fun, change something until you are. Decide what it is you are passionate about, and then pursue it with vigor. Keep your eyes open! Don't spend too much time sleeping. Once today is over, it is gone for good. Remember, the Deal of the Decade comes along about once a week. Find a couple for yourself. And most important of all, have some fun along the way!

Successful investing!

OTHER BOOKS
BY DOLF DE ROOS

101 Ways to Massively Increase the Value of Your Real Estate Without Spending Much Money

As suggested in Chapter 1, and explained in more detail in Chapter 12, not only does Dolf contend that there are 101 ways to massively increase the value of a property without spending much money on it, but true to form he sits down and details them in writing.

In this book, Dolf shares some obvious and some esoteric ways that you can easily increase the value of your property by far more than the cost of the improvement. If by spending $1,000 to build a carport, you increase the rental income of that property by $1,000 per year (which is a 100 percent return on your $1,000 investment), why would you not do it? Especially if, as Dolf shows you, you do not even have to come up with the $1,000 out of your own pocket in the first place.

You may not choose to implement all of the 101 ideas detailed in this book on one property, but there will be ideas here that you would never think of in a month of Sundays on your own. Why would you not implement at least some of them?

Extraordinary Profits from Ordinary Properties

For years, Dolf shared his experiences in the real estate market with people through his writings, his books, and his seminars. His success stories were so regular that people began to think that while it may be easy for *him*, it was not possible for *them* to achieve anywhere near the same sorts of results. Consequently, Dolf invited people on his database to submit photos and a brief description of properties they had bought, thinking that the submissions would lead to some interesting statistical analyses.

However, the stories that people submitted were so amazing, so enthralling, and so inspirational that Dolf essentially reproduced them verbatim to show how even ordinary properties can lead to extraordinary profits.

Originally written using examples from New Zealand, further editions are being compiled showing examples from other regions as well. Check out his Web site at www.dolfderoos.com for details on the latest editions.

About the Author

Dr. Dolf de Roos began investing in real estate as an undergraduate student. Despite going on to earn a Ph.D. in electrical and electronic engineering from the University of Canterbury, Dolf increasingly focused on his flair for real estate investing, which has enabled him to have never had a job. He has, however, invested in many classes of real estate (residential, commercial, industrial, hospitality, and specialist) all over the world.

Today he is the chairman of the public company Property Ventures Limited, an innovative real estate investment company whose stated mission is to massively increase stockholders' worth. Over the years, Dolf was cajoled into sharing his investment strategies, and he has run seminars on the Psychology of Creating Wealth and on Real Estate Investing throughout North America, Australia, New Zealand, Asia, the Middle East, and Europe since the 1980s.

Beyond sharing his investment philosophy and strategies with tens of thousands of investors (beginners as well as seasoned experts), Dolf has also trained real estate agents, written and published numerous bestselling books on property, and introduced computer software designed to analyze and manage properties quickly and efficiently. He often speaks at investors' conferences, real estate agents' conventions, and his own international seminars, and regularly takes part in radio shows and television debates. Born in New Zealand, raised in Australia, New Zealand, and Europe, Dolf, with six languages up his sleeve, offers a truly global perspective on

189

the surprisingly lucrative wealth-building opportunities of real estate.

To find out what you can learn from Dolf's willingness to share his knowledge about creating wealth through real estate, and to receive his free monthly newsletter, please visit his Web site at www.dolfderoos.com.

Index

Accounting, 144–145
Acquiring debt, 126
Advertisements:
    classified, 81–84
    writing own, 96–97
Agents, real estate, 88–95
Agrarian society, 55
Analyzing properties:
    by cash-on-cash return, 101–102
    by internal rate of return,
        102–106
    location and, 106
    as outsider, 107
    by yield, 101
Appraisal:
    by bank, 9, 11
    for depreciation write-off, 31
Arizona, 154
"As Nominee" phrase in contract,
    113
Asset:
    debt on appreciating, 126
    depreciating, 17, 24, 28–31
    property as, 15–17
Asset value, increases in, 19–22
Assignment of lease document,
    158–159
Auckland (New Zealand), 51, 53
Australia:
    changes in stock market and real
        estate values in, 37
    Gold Coast of, 184
    Queensland, 52, 53
    Sydney Wool Exchange, 162–163

Automation, 56
Averages:
    beating, 22
    demographics, beating through,
        53–54
    fluctuation around, 34–39,
        45–46
    geography, beating through,
        49–53
    lottery ticket and, 34
    overview of, 33–34
    seaside real estate, beating with,
        54–59

Baby boomers, 54, 57
Bankruptcy of companies,
    44
Banks:
    appraisal by, 9, 11
    borrowing from, 119, 120–121,
        126–127
    long-term leases and, 158
    See also Mortgages
Bargain properties:
    Deal of Decade, 179–180
    finding, 85–88
    reality of, 8–10
    reasons for existence of,
        10–12
Beating averages:
    through demographics, 53–54
    ease of, 22
    through geography, 49–53
    with seaside real estate, 54–59

Borrowing money:
  alternatives to 90 percent
    mortgages, 64
  to buy property, 5–6
  loan, asking bank manager for,
    120–121
  See also Loans; Mortgages; Other
    People's Money (OPM)
Broadbank (New Zealand),
  176
Buying property:
  capital required for, 160–164
  making money when, 174
  owner-sellers and, 81–82
  with zero or little down,
    177–178
Buying stock, 4–5

California:
  migration to, 52–53
  prices in, 50
  tenant laws in, 153–154
Candy stall, xvi
Capital gains tax, 15
Capital required to buy property,
  160–164
Care of property, 155–157
Carport example, 129–132
Cash-on-cash return:
  analyzing properties based on,
    101–102
  depreciation and, 30
  internal rate of return compared
    to, 83–84
Casinos, gambling at, 46–47
CDs (certificates of deposit),
  investing in, 20
Cities, growth of, 55–56
Classes of property:
  commercial, 152
  hospitality, 152–153

industrial, 152
  residential, 151–152
Classified advertisements, 81–84
College and success, xvi–xvii
Commercial property:
  capital required to buy, 160–164
  care of, 155–157
  description of, 152
  example of, 82–84
  increasing value of, 14, 132–133,
    134
  lease length for, 157–158
  loan-value ratios and, 164–165
  management overheads and, 164
  philosophical difference between
    residential property and,
    153–155
  rentals of, 155
  residential property compared to,
    166–168
  tenants, getting for, 158–160
Communications technology, 56
Companies, longevity of, and stock,
  40–41, 44
Comps (comparables), 39
Contract:
  "As Nominee" phrase in, 113
  commercial property and, 153,
    154–155
  legal out, language for, 114
  secrecy clause in, 114–115
  stapling check to, 115–117
  "suitable to himself" clause in,
    113–114
  writing items into, 111–113
  writing name on, 113
Credit Suisse First Boston, 162
Currency traders, 59–60

Deal, falling in love with, 175
Deal of Decade, 179–180

Debt, acquiring, 126
Demographics, beating averages
    through, 53–54
Depreciating asset, 17, 24, 28–31
Depreciation recapture tax, 28,
    65–66
Detractors, 18
Divorce and bargain property,
    10
Doctorate, earning, xviii

Earthquakes, 42–43
Eastern Europe, 184–185
Elderly, catering to, 54
Estate, settling property in, 11–12
Evictions, 145, 153–154
Excitement of real estate, 117
*Extraordinary Profits from Ordinary
    Properties* (de Roos), 188

Finance, finding sources of,
    120–121
Financial intelligence, developing,
    67
Finding:
    bargain properties, 85–88
    real estate agents, 89–90
    sources of finance, 120–121
    tenants, 159–160
    tradesmen, 140
Finding property:
    agents, 88–95
    classified advertisements,
        81–84
    off-market sales, 95–96
    real estate magazines, 84–88
    sources of listings, 98–99
    writing own advertisements,
        96–97
Foreclosure situations, 11
Fruit stall, xvi

Funeral parlor example:
    contract with seller of, 110
    loan-value ratio and, 164–165
    reluctant real estate agent and,
        92–94
Futures contracts, 60

Gambling at casinos, 46–47
Gearing (leverage), 21
Geography, beating averages
    through, 49–53
Golden rules of property:
    be countercyclical, 176–177
    buy from motivated seller,
        174
    buy with zero or little down,
        177–178
    Deal of Decade comes along
        about once a week, 179–180
    fall in love with deal, not
        property, 175
    make money when buying, 174
    never name figure first, 175–176
    overview of, 173–174
    seldom sell, 178–179
Goodwill factor and business,
    158
Government:
    interference in market by,
        169–172
    requisition of property by, 42
Grain, going against, 176–177

Harcourts (New Zealand), 98–99
Hospitality property, 152–153

Increasing value of property:
    carport example, 129–132
    options for, 13–15, 133–135
    storage garage example,
        132–133

Industrial property, 152
Instant-payment system, 141–142
Instant results, expectations of, 13
Insurance, 42–43, 45, 64
Integrity, xvii–xviii
Interest-only mortgage, 122
Interest rate:
    on loans, 7
    on mortgages, as deductible, 22
Internal rate of return (IRR),
        analyzing properties based on,
        102–106
Interviewing tenants, 138–139
Investors:
    international market and,
        182–183
    real estate agents as, 89

Japan, 183
Job, stigma of not having, xv

Keeping eye on market, 59–61

Landlording, *see* Managing
    property
Landslides, 43
Lease and sale of business,
    158–159
Lease length, 157–158
Legal out of contract, language for,
    114
Leverage:
    mortgage financing and, 17, 21
    yields and, 24–25
Litigation, 111–112
Living by wits, 117
Loans:
    asking bank manager for,
        120–121
    interest rate on, 7
    See also Borrowing money

Loan-value ratios, 164–165
Location of property, 46, 106
Looking at properties:
    in more detail, 85
    100:10:3:1 Rule and, 73–79
Loss of property, 42–44
Lottery tickets, 34
Low of market, determining,
    177

Magazines, real estate, 84–88
Management overheads, 164
Managing property:
    accounting, 144–145
    evictions, 145, 153–154
    hiring property managers,
        145–147
    overview of, 137–138
    rule enforcement, 142–144
    tenant selection, 138–140
    tradesmen, finding, 140
    tradesmen, paying, 141–142
Margin, buying stocks on, 4–5
Market, keeping eye on, 59–61
Mentoring, 75–76, 89
Misrepresentations:
    of increases in asset values,
        19–22
    yields, 22–25
Money, borrowing:
    alternatives to 90 percent
        mortgages, 64
    to buy property, 5–6
    loan, asking bank manager for,
        120–121
    See also Loans; Mortgages;
        Other People's Money
        (OPM)
Monopoly (game), 181–182
Mortgage guarantee insurance,
    64

Mortgage lenders, 121
Mortgages:
    classes of, 121–123
    interest rate on, as deductible, 22
    90 percent type, 63–64
    paying off, 123–125
    proposal for finance and,
        122–123
Muldoon, Sir Robert, 171

Naming figure in negotiations,
    175–176
Negotiations:
    concepts for, 113–115
    creativity and, 110–111
    naming figure in, 175–176
    poker compared to, 117
    restaurant example, 111–113
    seductive offer, making,
        115–117
    See also Offering
Netherlands, 64, 171
Newport Property Ventures, viii
New Zealand:
    Auckland, 51, 53
    Broadbank, 176
    Harcourts, 98–99
    investing in, 183–184
    Queenstown property example,
        85–88
    rent freeze in, 171
90 percent mortgages, 63–64
Numbers game:
    investing in property as, 73, 76
    life as, vii–viii
    roulette and, 46–48
    stocks and, 48–49

Offering:
    to buy property, 96–97
    less than asking price, 83

stapling check to contract,
    115–117
    See also Negotiations
Off-market sales, 95–96
100:10:3:1 Rule, 73–79
*101 Ways to Massively Increase the
    Value of Your Real Estate
    Without Spending Much Money*
    (de Roos), 134, 187
Options trading, 60
Other People's Money (OPM):
    buying property using, 119–120
    finding sources of, 120–121
Outsider, viewing property as,
    107
Owner-sellers, 81–82

Passion, importance of, vii–viii
Paying off mortgages, 123–125
Paying tradesmen, 141–142
Perception as reality, 13–14
Perseverance and competition,
    94
Principal and interest mortgage,
    121–122
Private mortgage insurance (PMI),
    64
Property:
    as asset, 15–17
    averages and, 46
    as best investment, 3–4, 17–18
    buying and leveraging, 5–8
    depreciation allowance on, 29
    reasons to invest in, 69–70
    stability of, 41
    worth of, 8–12
Property Investor School, 175
Property managers, 145–147
Property market, 169, 171–172
Property Ventures Limited, 189
Proposal for finance, 122–123

Queenstown property example, 85–88

Real Estate Acquisition Program (REAP) software, 106
Real estate agents, 88–95
Real estate magazines, 84–88
Real Estate Management System (REMS) software, 144
Real estate market, 169, 171–172
Redevelopment of site, 43
References on tenants, 139
Refinancing, 16–17
Rental income, 15–16
Rentals, 155
Rent-rise restrictions, 169–171
Republic Tower, 161–162
Residential property:
  capital required to buy, 160–164
  care of, 155–157
  commercial property compared to, 166–168
  description of, 151–152
  increasing value of, 129–132
  lease length for, 157–158
  loan-value ratios and, 164–165
  management overheads and, 164
  philosophical difference between commercial property and, 153–155
  rentals of, 155
  tenants, finding for, 159–160
Restaurant example, 111–113
Retirement needs, 54, 57
Return on property investment, 22–25
Rich, study of, xvii–xviii
Risk and interest rates, 7
Robbins, Tony, 67

Roulette, 46–48
Rule enforcement with tenants, 142–144
Rules and regulations of transactions, 109–110

Safety of investment in property, 7
Sales, off-market, 95–96
Search criteria, narrowing down, 77–78
Seaside real estate, 54–59
Secrecy clause in contract, 114–115
Security of investment in property, 7
Seductive offer, making, 115–117
Selecting:
  property managers, 147
  tenants, 138–140
  tradesmen, 140
Sellers, buying from motivated, 174
Selling:
  property, 178–179
  stocks, 15
Sensitivity analysis, 105
Shops, block of, example, 90–92
Software:
  accounting, 144
  to determine internal rate of return, 104–106
Standard deviation, 38
Stapling check to contract, 115–117
Stocks:
  Australia, growth statistics in, 37
  buying, 4–5
  fluctuations around average and, 37–38, 39–40, 45
  longevity of companies and, 40–41, 44
  market, keeping eye on, 60

numbers game and, 48–49
portfolio, increasing value of,
12–13
prediction and, 52
selling, 15
U.S., growth statistics in,
35–36
worth of, 8
Storage garage example, 132–133
Success and college, xvi–xvii
"Suitable to himself" clause in
contract, 113–114
Sydney Wool Exchange, 162–163

Tasmania, 52
Tax laws, 27–31
Tenants:
for commercial property,
158–159
evicting, 145, 153–154
finding, 159–160
rent-rise restrictions and,
169–171
rules, enforcing, 142–144
selecting, 138–140

Tradesmen:
finding, 140
paying, 141–142
Transactions, rules and regulations
of, 109–110

Value of property:
carport example, 129–132
increases in, 19–22
options for increasing, 13–15,
133–135
standard deviation and, 38
storage garage example,
132–133
Visiting prospective tenants,
139–140

Worth of property, 86
Writing:
advertisements, 96–97
items into contract, 111–113
Written-down book value, 28

"Yes, but" brigade, 66–67
Yields, 22–25, 101

How to take advantage of resources available to create wealth through real estate

With real estate, as with most other activities in life, you cannot hope to learn all you need to know by reading one book once. Although real estate is far more stable, consistent, and dependable than many other financial activities, keeping up with trends and ahead of the competition is imperative. Read many books on the subject (the book you don't read cannot help you!), attend seminars, talk with other investors, and dream up your own ideas to try out in the marketplace.

Success leaves clues! We have a number of resources to help both aspiring and seasoned investors. Please visit our Web site at www.dolfderoos.com to find out about our:

Books
Tape Sets
Software
Mentoring Programs
Seminar Schedules
New Products, Services, and Events

Finally, remember that contrary to the saying "knowledge is power," it is only *applied* knowledge that is power. It is not enough to know a lot about real estate—to achieve real estate riches, you must put the theories into action. It's the difference between being interested and being committed.

Subscribe to our Free Monthly Newsletter

We trust that the resources available on our Web site at www.dolfderoos.com will empower you and propel you on your way to not needing (or wanting!) a job thanks to real estate.